Flipping
Confidential

Flipping Confidential

The Secrets of Renovating Property for Profit in Any Market

Kirsten Kemp

John Wiley & Sons, Inc.

Published by John Wiley & Sons, Inc., Hoboken, New Jersey.

Published simultaneously in Canada.

Wiley Bicentennial Logo: Richard J. Pacifico

For general information on our other products and services or for technical support, please contact our Customer Care Department within the United States at (800) 762-2974, outside the United States at (317) 572-3993 or fax (317) 572-4002.

Wiley also publishes its books in a variety of electronic formats. Some content that appears in print may not be available in electronic books. For more information about Wiley products, visit our web site at www.wiley.com.

Library of Congress Cataloging-in-Publication Data:

Kemp, Kirsten.
    Flipping confidential : the secrets of renovating property for profit in any
market / Kirsten Kemp.
       p.   cm.
    ISBN 978-0-470-06835-9 (pbk.)
    1. Flipping (Real estate investment)   2. House selling.   3.
Dwellings—Maintenance and repair.   I. Title.
    HD1382.5.K46   2007
    332.63'243—dc22

                                                         2007000436

Printed in the United States of America.

10   9   8   7   6   5   4   3   2   1

To Dad
who started me on this flipping journey
and Mom, Walker, Nola, and EO
with whom I still get to share it.

Contents

◈ CONTENTS ◈

Acknowledgments

Mom, I admire your iron gut and will always be grateful for your endless support. Dad, your spirit comforts me with its quiet strength. I miss you. Thank you, Clem Blake for your unwavering goodness and witty flipitisms; my dear and talented friend Jenna McCarthy, without whom this book would not have been written; and Matt McAllister for introducing me to Jenna and allowing me to shamelessly plug my various antics on your radio show. Kathy Lymberopoulos for your loyalty and leadership; Diane DeMartino for telling me to write a book; Tracy Verna for making it possible; Laurie Harting for showing me the ropes; Brian Knappenberger for your keen eye; Kim Prince for anticipating my every need; and Elizabeth Ford for understanding the needs of another working mom. Thank you, Darrell Becker, for sharing your knowledge, attention to detail and for your guidance, Mary Belle Snow for giving me the confidence to jump in, Gina Brogi for your unwavering friendship, and Malek Doulat for your insight and smarts. To Renee Grubb and Ed Edick, who let me keep a desk at the office even when I'm not focused on selling a ton of real estate; Laina Mayfield-Condron for your informative loan contributions; Diana MacFarlane for your mortgage expertise; Jane Hilty for your escrow excellence; Pete Slaughter for your reliable legal jargon; Erin Chrislock for your negotiating talents, patience, and clarity. Greg Maher for crunching the numbers and keeping me accountable. To Tomas Ramirez for telling me not to worry, we can do it! and to Teresa Uribe because your unflappable work ethic and steadfastness inspire me and help me maintain my perspective. There are countless contractors, vendors, stores, subcontractors, clients, and friends who have supported me along this journey. You have all touched me and influenced this book in one way or another, and I thank you—Brianna, Erin, Khasy, Joy, Laura, Geof, Sandee, Gil, Valerie, Lisa, Nancy, Prem, Carter, Alberta, AJ, Richie, Gina, Janie, Jay, Karen, Pat, Jason, James, Gene, Kim, Joele, Kevin, Derek, Joey, Jorge, Jose Luis, Salvador, Efrain, Miguel, Juan, Jesus, Jerry, Erica, Forrest, Nate, Alicia, Brett, Lenci, Christy, Maddy, Scott, Christine, Geoff, Sandy, Steve, Max, Betsy, Al, Joe Coito, and Starbucks for keeping me awake long enough to finish this book but perhaps not alert enough to include everyone who deserves to be mentioned here. Finally, my heartfelt thanks to my family for making everything more worthwhile.

1

INTRODUCTION

Flip·i·tis (flip-ˊī-tis) *n.*   Addiction to buying, fixing, and selling houses for profit.

No cocktail party conversation would be complete without the whispered mention of some mutual acquaintance who has just made a fortune buying and selling a house. When talk turns to profit, the numbers sound like Monopoly money to you: Are these people really making more money in 8 or 12 weeks than you make all year? You can't help but fantasize—there you are, working for yourself (swinging a hammer like nobody's business, I might add), creating extraordinary living spaces, and becoming wealthy beyond your wildest dreams in the process. What's not to like about that particular scenario? But then you remember: You have no experience, no money, and no applicable skills.

I have some good news for you. There's an art and a science to flipping houses, and it doesn't take an engineering degree and a bottomless trust fund to do it. Several years ago, I had a real estate client, Lety, who purchased her first condo in Santa Barbara for $200,000, 110 percent of which was borrowed. Because she had no money whatsoever, she even had to borrow the cash to cover her closing costs. Lety was a single mom who desperately wanted to provide security for her young son. Although she didn't have a penny to her name, she was employed full-time as a hairdresser and had a loyal, steady clientele. She possessed an inspirational resolve and an innate understanding that the key to financial independence was to invest in real estate even though, technically, she had nothing to invest.

Because Lety's funds to get into her home didn't come out of pocket, her mortgage payment was steep. Lety made many sacrifices to keep that condo, but she never complained because she had her eye on the prize: building equity and, hence, financial stability for her future, for her son. While she was living there, Lety made some minor cosmetic changes to her condo—replaced linoleum with tile, painted, and changed out some light fixtures and hardware. Two years later, she sold it for $298,000, a healthy profit in any market. She dropped $325,000 on her next condo, made similar improvements (and sacrifices to keep it), and sold it 18 months later for $435,000. With the equity she had acquired, Lety partnered with her sister and bought a house for $950,000, completely overhauled it, and sold it 16 months later for $1,175,000. They split their profits, and Lety purchased a single-family residence in need of her now well-honed special touch. There was a nice yard for her and her son, and she is now enjoying the comforts of well-deserved stability.

Think about this scenario. Here's a single mom with no money and limited skills. Lety struggled to get into a $200,000 condo, and just five years later, she was dabbling in million-dollar deals. Did she set out to become a "flipper?" Probably not. Was it easy? No. Scary at times? No doubt. Worth the sacrifice? Absolutely.

Lety didn't have experience or cash, but she did have what it takes to be a successful flipper: a principled conscience, an iron gut, a keen sense of organization, a passion for the process, a healthy dose of reality, and a finely honed sense of humor. That last bit is key. Take it from me—someone who's lost (and made) more money in 12 years than some people see in a lifetime—because there is no better backdrop for raucous laughter than a construction site under a self-imposed time crunch. Of course, how long and how heartily you chuckle (and how quickly you recover) will depend on your mind-set, attitude, and perspective—all of which we'll be sure to get in the right place before you begin your flipping journey.

Let's say you meet the basic criteria: You're a ballsy yet pragmatic control freak who's interested in real estate and, on occasion, has brought the house down with a well-timed one-liner. But how can you really know if flipping houses is for you? First, you must determine what your goals are and, perhaps more important, what they aren't. If you want to find a creative outlet and leave your stamp on the world of decorating, go to design school and enjoy making the world a more beautiful place, one grass-cloth covered wall at a time. If you dream of overhauling something unsightly—overnight—get yourself a nice garage sale umbrella stand and a can of spray paint and call it a day. If you want to have scads of money but don't really want to work all that hard, find yourself a willing benefactor and spend your days watching football or popping bonbons.

But, if you want to be your own boss (not just finally tell the one you currently have where to go), you're in the right place. If you want to spend more time on vacation and less time punching the clock, keep reading. If you're looking for more time with your family and less hours behind a desk, don't skip a word. If you want to be an efficient, professional leader of a team with a common goal, don't put this book down. If you know without a doubt that you have fantabulous taste and want to test-drive your creative ideas on a house that you won't necessarily want to call home (but would be willing to live in if push came to shove), get a highlighter. If you want a sense of accomplishment unlike any other you've felt before, start taking notes. If you want to increase your wealth because of what it will make of you and do for you, and not just for money, get ready to sit down to a banquet of information.

Even if you're a complete novice, don't be daunted. Like anything worthwhile, flipping properties is hard work that happens to have untold side benefits. Beyond making you wealthy and wise, your new hobby will almost certainly teach you more about yourself than you ever thought you wanted to know.

Because here's the thing: This flipping business is a journey, and the destination is probably not the one you had in mind when you first picked up this book. Just about everyone I've ever met who's been desperate to get into this game has had dollar signs where pupils should be. I'd be flat-out lying if I told you I started turning houses for altogether altruistic reasons. I was raised by frugal parents who thought that brand-new clothing was a luxury and that coupons and toilet paper were winning Christmas gifts. We weren't poor, but we didn't spend much money either. If I received an expensive present or we went anywhere fancy, it was because my parents—particularly my dad—knew how to finagle a deal.

We traveled a lot when I was growing up—mostly performing as a family. My Dad a concert pianist, my Mom a singer with the voice of an angel, and I rounded out the trio with my singing, dancing, fluting, and guitar-playing so together we were sort of the scaled-down Von Trapps and I ached to have the glamorous things I saw in far-off places. I wanted to buy designer clothes and drive a luxurious car. But I also wanted the freedom that money could bring. I wanted the good life. I didn't want to have to worry about mundane things like retirement accounts and mortgages. I wanted to feel secure. After my maiden stint in the first-class cabin of an airplane, scored by Dad simply walking up to the ticketing agent and "volunteering" to be bumped up, I vowed never again to fold my elongated frame into a miniscule coach seat. Little did I know these experiences were shaping my future.

Yes, money allows you to make even more money. And if that's all you're interested in, that's fine; skip ahead to Chapter 7 to learn all about the mechanics of a flip, and repeat until you master the fine art of flipping. But I'll let you in on a little secret: Whoever said that money can't buy happiness never helped a penniless single mother purchase her first home and make more money in equity in just a few weeks than she had made in her entire lifetime. Whoever thinks poverty builds character (or affluence annihilates it) never saw the look of pride on that mother's face the first time she fixed lunch for her family on the countertop she had helped install or pulled a load of clothes out of the dryer she had paid for with her own earnings.

Anyone can make money. And as much as our society might have you believe otherwise, money isn't the answer to all your problems. There are enough miserable millionaires to fill a stadium. It is what having money makes *of you* that counts at the end of the day. Beyond fattening your bank account, flipping houses can give you the power to transform lives—your own and those around you. Get yourself a tasty beverage and find a comfy place to read, because I'm here to tell you how to do both.

The rest of this book details the highs and lows of the series of home sales that have occupied the past decade of my life. I explain where I made money, where I lost it, and precisely how much. I share stories of royal screwups, as well as every single painful but necessary lesson I learned along the way. I describe how this business has made me a better mother, daughter, neighbor, employer, and friend.

First, a note about semantics: For the sake of ease and clarity, I use the term *flipper* to refer to any person trying to make money by buying, rehabilitating, and selling a house for profit in the least amount of time. It is an industry term that we use on the television series *Property Ladder*, so it's an unconscious part of my vocabulary. I know what you're thinking because I've heard it before: Flipper was a dolphin. You, of course, are no one's pet porpoise. You are a Real Estate Rejuvenator, a Realty Recycler, a Residential Resuscitator. Nothing negative is implied by the word flipper as I use it here. In some circles, however, the word has dubious connotations. Case in point: When other Realtors or neighbors hear of your plans, they may state (not ask) with no small amount of contempt, "So, you're just gonna *flip* it." You will likely see, if not actually feel, the spittle coming from their lips as they deliver this line. They are implying that you are going to cheap out, do the least amount of real work possible, hide as many problems as you can, use cut-rate materials, and walk away with a pocketful of cash. I don't really need to say it, but I will: That is not what we are trying to do here.

If you are going to be buying and selling houses for a profit, if you are willing to gamble your money, spend your precious time comparing fixtures and finishes, run a crew, manage the most tedious of accounting jobs, put out an endless string of fires, and generally work your ass off, you deserve to be handsomely compensated. You are still a flipper, but in the best possible sense of the word: someone who takes a neglected and outdated space and polishes it into something attractive and desirable.

For sure, there are some flippers out there who do things on the fly—they continually cut corners, do shoddy work, use inferior products, maybe even treat their crews deplorably—and still make obscene amounts of money. They are sometimes called "lick and stick" or "fix and flip" experts and they are why flipping occasionally gets a bad rap. They may lug home a hefty paycheck now and again, but over time buyers find them out. Are lenders, real estate agents, and subcontractors willing to work with them again? *Do they sleep at night?*

You and I didn't create this opportunity, but the reality is that there are many buyers out there who don't have the time, skills, or interest to get personally involved in the fix-up business, and they're willing to pay a premium not to have to do it. It is really not so different from going out to eat. My guess is that you are probably capable of reading a recipe, shopping for a prescribed list of ingredients, opening and closing the oven, and cleaning up all by yourself. But sometimes for whatever reason—you don't have it in you, you've got other things to do, the dog ate your apron—you choose to pop into a restaurant and have your meal catered. Blissful, no? Do you think you're being scammed just because you could have done it yourself but chose not to? As long as the experience is a good one, everyone wins. On the other hand, if your meal, the service, or the atmosphere was miserable, the eatery in question is not likely to get your business again (and you're likely to tell anyone who will listen about your bout of botulism/surly server/rodent-sighting experience).

The bottom line is, don't be that guy (or gal). Do the job right and you can wear your flipperhood proudly. Do it for the right reasons and I promise you that you will experience a kind of wealth you can't even fathom yet. With enough folks like you and me in the game, eventually the term flipper might even begin to be seen as positive. Dare I even hope, complimentary?

Another note about terminology: I'm a modern gal, and I try my best to be politically correct. I know that men are nurses and women are neuroscientists. However, this book would be a miserable, tedious read if I had to say "he or she" every time I referred to a lender, buyer, seller, contractor, or real estate agent. It disrupts the flow of thought. So I alternate using pronouns such as he/she, him/her, his/hers, but unless I indicate otherwise, either gender is meant; the appropriate pronouns are interchangeable.

I'm a flipper. I can say that with confidence and pride. If you'd like to be a flipper, too—if you're ready to enrich not just your bottom line but your entire life—read on.

2

MY STORY

Flip·per (ˊflip-ər) *n.*   A person who tries to buy, rehabilitate, and sell real estate for profit. Or a dolphin.

If you are reading this book, chances are that you've either seen the television show *Property Ladder,* or someone you know recommended *Flipping Confidential* to you. Maybe Aunt Betty gave it to you as a birthday present because she thinks you are hiding your inner designer. Maybe you stumbled on it in a bookstore purely by accident and began thumbing through it out of curiosity. Whatever the case, now that you're in possession of these pages you are probably wondering if and how I'm qualified to dispense advice on buying, fixing, and selling houses.

As I describe in detail in the following chapters, I've flipped houses enough times to land a TV show on the topic and, in fact, earn a nice living. Eventually, I could no longer ignore the constant requests to put my experiences down on paper. This is not all gratuitous boasting, I promise. (The truth is that my mistakes have been many and profound.) My hope is that by sharing my rent-to-own story and explaining what buying and selling homes has done for me personally and professionally, you may be inspired to jump into the flip game with minimum pain and maximum gain.

Now you may be asking yourself why I should care about you and your happiness. Part of the reason is admittedly selfish. The whole real estate industry (not just the handful of crooked flippers out there) often gets a bad rap. And since real estate is my career, I have a vested interest in changing the perception that anyone who makes money off of your money has to be a shark, right? And folks who talk in absolutes ("This house will never sell at that price") cannot be trusted. People who feel the need to put their mug on every ad, business card, flyer, and sign they use are more interested in ego aggrandizement than personalized service. (I tend to agree with that assessment, although the industrywide belief is that recognition builds trust.) The truth is, Realtors have a tedious and time-consuming job, and if they are doing it well, they deserve every penny they earn.

But there is a bigger motivation for sharing my story. People ponder the question constantly: "Can you really have it all?" Who has it all—The former supermodel with a zest for life; a designer home; attentive spouse; well-mannered kids; ample time for her philanthropic passion; a massage and facial in the middle of the day, if she wants one; and of course, a job that she looks forward to most days even though she doesn't need the money?

So what is having it all? The simplicity of having your basic needs met with a little extra on the side, maybe. There's a book I read to my kids that illustrates my point. It's called *The Rainbow Fish* (North South Books, 1992) and stars a flashy little fellow who happens to be covered in gorgeous, glittery scales. The Rainbow Fish knows that he is more beautiful than his oceanmates and snickers when they ask him to share his gilded gills. He is so much better than they are! Why should he share with the likes of them? And if he did give away his scales, why, he wouldn't be better than them at all! So for a while, he chooses superiority over popularity. (I'm sure you can see where this is going.) Eventually, loneliness trumps vanity and he grudgingly gives away a scale. And then another. And yet another. Although he is becoming less glamorous with each offering, his happiness is growing exponentially. He has friends! The other fish like him! Alas, it was only in giving away what he had that he learned its true value.

Okay, it's a little simplistic. But it's a sweet story with a nice message. Before you get all exasperated, let's get something straight. I am in no way suggesting that you work your ass off to build yourself a nice nest egg and then donate it to the nearest mission. The money you make is yours to do with as you please. Spend it, save it, gamble it away, set it on fire for all I care. I am simply saying that material wealth can and will bring you more (joy, freedom, grief, anxiety) than you ever dreamed possible.

Money is power, and how you use that power can make or break your happiness. If you're miserable, chances are you

11

will make your family miserable. If you experience bliss, so will your family. I worked hard to find happiness and I want you to find it as well. Who knows? You could turn out to be my neighbor or my daughter's boss or my son's mother-in-law. You might be the paramedic who rescues my best friend from the mangled wreckage that until recently was her car, or the flight attendant who holds my mother's hand on the bumpy flight that's bringing her to her aunt's funeral. This world is a small place, and we're all in it together.

Starting Out as an Actress

Although I love helping people, I never wanted to be a pediatric cardiologist, never dreamed of being a social worker. I started my professional life as an actress—hardly the Mother Teresa School of Philanthropy. It wasn't any great passion for the craft of acting that prompted me to get a SAG (Screen Actors Guild) card, either. Like a lot of people, I found something I was good at and that came easily to me, so I did it. I know plenty of actors (and would-be actors) who believe with the utmost certainty that their life would be dull and meaningless if they weren't onstage or in front of the camera. Not me. That just was not my shtick. I liked the work, it was fun, I made good money, and it gave me the flexibility and the time to go to yoga and get the occasional facial. Under worked and overpaid—not a bad gig. But I probably was as passionate about the triple chai latte that I would pick up on my way to an audition as I was about actually landing any particular role.

Despite my lack of driving ambition, the roles came. Acting and performing have remained in my blood from the day

I first warbled "Do-Re-Mi" onstage at age 4; they are not going anywhere anytime soon. When opportunity knocks, I still take a flip hiatus to do a sitcom and give my blisters time to heal. I was double majoring in acting and music on a music scholarship (those flute lessons paid off) at Occidental College in a little suburb of Los Angeles when I landed roles on *Saved by the Bell* and *Head of the Class.* The acting department at Occidental was none too pleased. Apparently it did not want students doing professionally what the department was trying to teach. Rather than give up my income, I switched my majors to Spanish and French, not even realizing how useful the former would be in my future construction and real estate dealings. Once again, a seemingly benign decision turned out to be a secret weapon down the road.

Unleashing My Inner Designer

After a year of dorm living, I set myself up in a modest (okay, ugly) little one-bedroom apartment near campus and commenced decorating it. During the day, I'd work a little, maybe drop in on a Spanish or art history class, but outside school it was all about the crib. Keep in mind it was the mid-1980s, when black lacquer was all the rage and Patrick Nagel's sleek, minimalist models adorned every other wall in sight. Me? Long before shabby was chic, I was into doilies. Doilies everywhere. My boyfriend during sophomore year of college was a jock, but his mom was as crafty as they come. Georgene knew her way around a glue gun and every weekend while my boyfriend was swinging a baseball bat, his mom would teach me the arts of basket-weaving, sewing machine threading, and teddy bear making. I sucked it all up like paint on a roller. No matter what time of day or night you happened to stop by my pad, the antique mahogany dining table was set with elegant linens, gilt-edged chargers, and delicately carved crystal (true to my inherited nature, picked up at garage sales and secondhand stores or passed down from Grammy). My crummy hand-me-down TV, too ghastly to look at, was camouflaged with Con-Tact (adhesive paper) in an effort to make it blend into my cabbage-rose wallpaper. I sponge painted my way across wall after wall, sanded and stained an army of used furniture, experimented with crazy color combinations, arranged and rearranged my two-room Buckingham apartment until in my mind, it became a palace (its absence of majestic carved ceiling and marble tile flooring notwithstanding).

Ten years later, the whole world would be copying my then cutting-edge Paris Apartment style. But at the time, it was funky. Different. Friends began asking me to help them decorate their apartments and dorm rooms. My mom would ask, "How do you know how to *do* this stuff?" And the truth was that I didn't know how to do any of it. But I was struggling and resourceful and had found a relatively creative, reasonably healthy way to occupy my time and feel fulfilled. I also realized that environment influences mood and that if I had order and tranquility in my surroundings, I would have them in my life. That was a huge trigger for me. "Find what you love to do and the money will come." It is the parental career-advice standby (delivered mostly, children suspect, because said parents don't know what a binary engineer or neurolinguistic programmer is), but in my case, it was undeniably true.

While I was busy beautifying my granny-chic apartment, my newly divorced mom was giving her own nearby house a complete overhaul. I'd visit daily to share my unsolicited opinions on everything from the floor plan and paint colors to wall and window treatments. Finally, she threw me a bone— the basement was *mine* to do with as I pleased. The whole basement! *The whole dark, low-ceiling basement.* The understanding was that this little subterranean slice of heaven would be my home-back-home whenever I wanted or needed it. That being the case, the first thing that space needed was . . . space! Call me a prima donna, but seven-foot ceilings were simply too cramped for my six-foot-plus frame.

I will never forget the look on the contractor's face when I announced, "I guess we're going to have to lower the floor." Lower the floor? Well, raising the ceiling certainly wasn't an option since there happened to be an entire house above it. Therewith commenced my first taste of true hard labor. The concrete was jack hammered out, mountains of dirt were removed, we installed steel beams to support the changes and a new concrete pad was poured. It was a major deal. Lo and behold the floor was lowered and once again, magic ensued. Unlike at my own little apartment, I wasn't just decorating here, I was *designing*.

I created a bathroom, kitchen, and living area, and learned how to exploit even the tiniest nook and cranny. I made every inch count. If there was a foot of space between the back of the closet and the living room wall, I made a broom closet. No counter space in the kitchen? I installed a shelf for the microwave. Once I tasted the satisfaction of transforming a slab of concrete and squat ceilings into a fabulous, functional living space, I was hooked.

My next opportunity to build a nest was born out of tragedy. I had just graduated from college and was getting great acting work when my dad got sick. If someone had told me that at 22 I'd be putting my TV career on hold to care for my dying father, I would have shook my head in disbelief. But there I was, a one-woman hospice crew, watching the man I loved more than anything in the world slowly make his way out of it. That time with him was gut wrenching and life altering, and in the end, an incredible gift that I learned to appreciate only after years had gone by.

Becoming a Flipper

When my father died, he left behind one heartbroken daughter (I'm an only child), a small pile of debts, and a dated, dilapidated house in serious need of cosmetic love. Though there was debt attached to the house, I was the sole heir and shifting into survival mode, I knew I needed to sell his house and get top dollar for it. I had a garage sale, ripped up smelly carpets, and tore down faded wallpaper.

In gutting my dad's house, I came across a coaster he had kept on his desk. The inscription: "A penny saved is hardly enough." I paused long enough to ponder the sad irony of that truth; after all, he had been the poster boy for saving all his life, and in the end he still had a stinky house and hadn't enjoyed a dime of all he had saved—what was he waiting for? I went back to the job at hand, more determined than ever. I did most of the work myself—I tore down the dated wallpaper in the front hall, tore out the pungent pee-stained carpet in the living room, and took out half the clutter my dad had collected over the years. I took help from anyone who would offer it, and in a way, my labor and dedication to the task at hand became free therapy to get through the pain of my loss. When I sold that house, I made a nice little return of $30,000.

I was debating how I was going to spend my $30,000 profit when I found out the universe had other plans. My penny-pinching pop had stipulated that I not receive any money from his estate (such as it was) until I turned 35—which was light-years away in my mind. This was a man who had taught me to buy no-load funds at age 8. At the time, I was hurt and angry, but those feelings of frustration ultimately drove me to succeed. After all, I had learned that fixing houses could be profitable. And I was good at it.

Shortly after my dad's death, I bought my first condo, using some cash I had saved from acting gigs as a down payment and a $10,000 gift from Mom. The condo was part of a brand-new building, but instinctively I knew it could be better. I just couldn't stop myself from changing what was supposedly a finished product. I repainted walls, enclosed an outdoor patio, added a half bath, and built a rooftop deck that afforded ocean views. They were simple, relatively inexpensive fixes that earned me an extra $80,000 when I sold the condo three years later. (Note that condominium developments often have strict rules about permissible architectural changes. Before altering your property, be sure to get approval from the governing body of the development.)

Right around then, I met and married Robert, who was then into magazine publishing. He encouraged my real estate career wholeheartedly, and soon we were orchestrating deals together. We bought our first house on our honeymoon, a $605,000 fixer-upper in Santa Barbara's ritzy sister city, Montecito (a slice of heaven and home to Oprah, Kathy Ireland, and Kenny Loggins, to name a few). This was also when I met Darrell Becker, the contractor who eventually would become a trusted friend and business partner. Robert and I invested $20,000 into our 1907 craftsman bungalow for some cosmetic renovations and listed it two years later . . . *for $839,000.* We simply took down a single-wall construction divider and expanded the living room. We painted the interior and added some retro shelves in the kitchen. With our furniture in the house (this is where I learned the value of staging, as I had collected beautiful craftsman antiques over the years I had owned this craftsman house), it looked warm and inviting, updated but still authentic and full of character. The money we pocketed was not bad for a few months' work, and it gave us the confidence to do it again. The hardest part about leaving that house was moving away from our fabulous neighbors—a challenge I would repeatedly face with future flips. After listening to the third or fourth confused neighbor (why would you buy that awful house, make it fabulous, borrow a cup of sugar, and then sell it?), I finally learned it was better to detach from the lovely homeowners with whom I shared a street, because settling in, receiving a welcome pie, and leaving shortly thereafter created a layer of emotional stress I just couldn't bear.

By this point, I was a bona fide flipper, but I didn't know it. I never went to design school (a fact I used to try to hide; now I'm proud of my self-taught skills), although I did work for the wildly talented clothing and interior designer Mary Belle Snow. She helped me get my eye in tune with color and design. I also had my mom's support, both with finances and in the search for unique architectural elements to incorporate into the homes I fixed up. She spent hours on eBay trying to score me deals. By the time I had bought and sold my 10th house, people were hiring me to help them renovate and design their personal and investment properties. Between acting, flipping, and designing, I found myself having to turn away work.

18

Some people would call it luck. But I prefer to repeat the old saying: The harder I work, the luckier I get. I have a theory that where preparedness meets opportunity, that's luck. When my manager saw the description for the part of the *Property Ladder* host (on-camera *and* design experience, flips properties, real estate license a plus), she knew it was the perfect role for me. I knew that I had a lot to say, and that I wanted to teach other people to be successful at something that had brought me so much satisfaction. But I also wanted to live in Santa Barbara and raise my family. Fortunately, I can do both. And in the past two years, I have also helped my housekeeper, her sister, and some of my crew acquire homes of their own. To me, that's having it all.

Here's where I often hear a collective "Hrmph." As in, "That's easy for *her* to say." You're busy, right? And the last time you checked, there were no money trees growing in your backyard. You're working a full-time job, maybe two—and you can't afford to quit to see where this journey takes you. That's the beauty of the flipping business: If you're smart and passionate and master some vital delegation and time-management skills, *you can be successful at this.* I'm a mom with two children (ages 3 and 5), a national TV show, a design business, and a gaggle of real estate and design clients. I have sat on the boards of countless charities and nonprofit organizations, and I volunteer my time at my kids' schools whenever I get the chance. It's a balancing act, and some days I'm better at it than others. But I love what I do, and I love the satisfaction I feel when I do a great job. I want you to have that, too.

Taming the flipping beast is just the first of my goals for both of us. Balancing life and flipping is hard, and doing it with grace is even harder. I strive every day to fully enjoy and appreciate and embrace all that I've been blessed with. I wish I could tell you there's a chapter on this, but in all honesty, I still haven't figured it out. If and when you do, I would love to hear all about it.

On a final note, I offer this disclaimer: When I hang up the other hats I juggle for their much-needed holiday and attempt to focus on flipping a house or two, I rely on my expertise as a designer and a Realtor. I am not a lender or a lawyer or a contractor or a plumber. I am confident that this book, which is a compilation of my knowledge and experiences, will answer at least a good chunk of your questions and get you started on the road to success. Alas, I cannot possibly address every possible scenario or query (although I have tried to include the most common questions people ask). Home prices can range from next to nothing to tens of millions of dollars. Tax and real estate laws and regulations vary from state to state. And buyers and sellers bring their own unique strengths, concerns, and neuroses into each sale. Therefore, there will be occasions throughout this book when my best advice will be: *Talk to an expert.* That's not a cop-out; that's me telling you what I would do.

I offer you my heartfelt congratulations on your decision to explore this exciting new world. I wish you enormous happiness on your journey.

3

GETTING STARTED

Flip·bot·o·my (flip-ˈbät-ə-mē) *n.*   The sinking feeling that you might have lost your mind when you first decided to embark on this journey.

Dear Kirsten,

I am a single mother with $13,000 in credit card debt. I work nights as a nurse and take care of four kids during the day. I have no savings and know nothing about construction, but I've seen your show *Property Ladder* and really want to make a career out of flipping houses. How do I start?

Of all the e-mail that I receive, "How do I get started?" is hands down the question I get asked most often. (It's right up there with "Can I borrow some cash for my first flip?") You may think my reply to the preceding letter went something along the lines of "Get your act together and get back to me." But anyone who has enough chutzpah to write that e-mail—or enough interest to pick up this book, for that matter—might well have what it takes to be successful in the flipping biz. How badly you want it and how much risk you are willing to take may not be as important as already being a Realtor and having an excellent credit score, but they factor into the equation nonetheless.

I wish I could say there was a checklist for determining your real estate readiness, but this ain't blackjack ("17, you hold; 16, you hit"). The first question you have to ask yourself is how much profit you need to make for a deal to be worthwhile. If your day job brings in $18,000 a year and you think by flipping a house you could make $3,000 for a month's work, it would probably be a smart move. If one month turned into six and the profit went down to $1,500 (or you broke even or *lost* money), would it still be wise? That depends on your goals, needs, and expectations. What if you learned a lot, the house turned out better than you'd even hoped, and you made some great contacts along the way, but you have no food in the fridge? These are questions only you can answer, but I urge you to think about precisely how much you're willing to sacrifice before applying for a loan or assembling a crew.

Once you have a rough idea of your profit requirements and risk profile, it is time to become familiar with the real estate market in your area. Bored, rich housewives likely being the exception and not the rule, most first-time flippers will probably be less than loaded starting off and therefore will need to focus on the area's entry-level homes or condos. Study your paper's real estate section, go to as many open houses as you can and ask lots of questions when you're there:

- How long has this house been on the market?
- What was the original asking price?
- What are comparable homes selling for (not listing at)?
- How many homes are on the market at or around this asking price?

The goal is to find an undervalued house and jump on it. Many real estate agents—especially if they think they might one day get your business—will happily hand over reams of valuable information along these very lines. Talk to as many as you can, take notes, and start a file. The more information you have, the more quickly you will spot that diamond in the rough you're looking for.

Finding the Money to Buy Your First Flip

On the universal Hottie Scale, Bo Derek was a "10." (Still is, in fact.) In the home-buying game, your attractiveness to lenders is measured by your FICO score. (FICO is an acronym for Fair Isaac Corporation, the company that created and standardized the credit risk scale.) The numbers vary slightly, but in general FICO scores range from 300 (yikes) to 850 (way to go). Somewhere between 620 and 660 seems to be the cutoff point for the best loans. If you're going to be borrowing a sum of seven digits or more, lenders usually like to see a score over 700.

Because your score is a product of your credit habits and history, it affects how much money you can borrow (or how much of a down payment you will need to come up with), how much it will cost you (in interest) to borrow it, and what types of loan will be available to you.

Knowing your FICO score is critical. "But it's . . . really, really bad," you whimper. So be it. Just as your doctor doesn't create an illness when she diagnoses it, exposing that number doesn't make your score what it is. It is already out there—and you need to know what it is (and do something about it if it is dreadful). Your credit score is only part of the picture when you are applying for a loan (the loan-to-value, or how much you're putting down on the property, is another biggie), but it is an important part and you need to be educated about it.

 Toolbox

By law, you are entitled to one free credit file disclosure (report) every 12 months from each of the three consumer credit reporting companies, Equifax, Experian, and TransUnion. You can request all three at www.annualcreditreport.com or by calling 1-877-322-8228. You can also contact each of the three reporting companies directly (at www.equifax.com, www.experian.com, and www.transunion.com).

Afraid that by checking out your credit, you might accidentally "ding" it? According to myFICO (www.myfico.com), an expert resource, your own credit report requests, credit checks made by businesses to offer you goods or services, or inquiries made by businesses with whom you already have a credit account do not affect your FICO score. Credit checks by prospective employers also do not count. These inquiries may appear on your credit report, but they do not have any bearing on your score.

There is only one type of credit inquiry that counts toward your FICO score. When you apply for a mortgage, auto loan, or other credit, you authorize the lender to request a copy of your credit report. These inquiries appear on your credit report and are included in your FICO score. However, multiple inquiries from auto or mortgage lenders within a short period are treated as a single inquiry and will have only a minor effect on your score.

If your FICO score rocks, you're good to go. But if that number is mediocre, miserable, or MIA (missing in action), you're going to need some help. Having no credit score can be as harmful as having a lousy one. Were you raised to be the credit-leery, cash-only type? That is fine and dandy—if you never want to purchase anything more extravagant than a toaster. Now is not the time to be idealistic or moralistic; it is time to get a credit card. I'm sure you've seen the slew of commercials plugging "personal bankers." Did you ever wonder what they were talking about? Now you'll know. A sharp personal banker—someone who knows the ins and outs of your financial life—will be your greatest ally during this entire process. If you don't already have this weapon stashed in your arsenal, this is a great opportunity to develop that relationship.

Establish Your Credit

Pay a visit to the branch where you keep your checking or savings account and explain your situation. If you don't connect with the first person to whom you pitch your ambitions, come back the next day. And the next. Be picky, but practical. Remember, *you need to establish credit.* And even if you get a card tomorrow, a lender will usually want to see at least six months of activity before forking over any dough. That means you actually have to use the card.

With no history of good behavior behind you, your only option may be a secured credit card, which is basically the "pay it forward" plan of the credit world: For example, you give the bank $500, and then you use your new-best-plastic-friend to pay for purchases up to that amount. It may seem pointless, but consistency and timeliness on your part help prove to potential lenders that you are financially responsible.

If you are approved for a nonsecured card, don't worry about exorbitant interest rates; you are not going to carry a balance anyhow. You are simply going to use the card where you formerly would have used cash or a check, and pay off the balance in full every month. If you're afraid you're going to find yourself in a pinch at the end of the billing cycle, you can set aside an equal amount of cash each time you say, "Charge it!" Envision every underwear purchase, every round of miniature golf with the kids, every podiatric copayment putting you one step closer to your ultimate goal. It is a visual tactic that can make an otherwise wearisome waiting process infinitely more enjoyable.

Clean Up Your Act

Now, if you're the guy who only wishes he didn't have a credit score, you've got some work to do. Sit down with your credit report and look at what's contributing to your rotten rating. Maybe it is less a product of late or nonpayment than what creditors call "debt potential." Remember when you were buying those sale-rack jeans, and the department store clerk asked you if you wanted to *save 10 percent right now on your purchase?* Remember how you said yes, and you filled out the little form and the skies opened up and they granted you a card on the spot? Well that action could be messing up your credit even if you never used the card once it was mailed to you.

You may not even have any idea how many credit cards you have, but if the preceding scenario sounds at all familiar, you could have dozens. Let's say you have 30 cards. If each card has a credit limit of $7,500, your *debt potential* is $225,000. Potential lenders weigh that number as carefully as any outstanding balances you might be carrying. Yes, debt potential can do you in.

What to do? Start making phone calls. These conversations may go a bit like this:

YOU: "Yes, I'm calling because I'd like to close this account."

PERSON WHOSE JOB IT IS TO KEEP YOU FROM CLOSING YOUR ACCOUNT: "Why, I'm sorry to hear that. And actually, it's quite fortunate that you happened to call today. As a special one-day-only promotion, we're going to waive any finance charges for the next 18 months . . ."

YOU (INTERRUPTING POLITELY): "Thanks just the same, but I would like to close this account *today.*"

PERSON WHOSE JOB IT IS TO KEEP YOU FROM CLOSING YOUR ACCOUNT: "Okay, then. We'll just get started here. Right after I tell you about our special Buyer Protection Plan—"

YOU (STRUGGLING TO REMAIN POLITE): "Again, thanks. But I'd like to close this account. *Now.* Can you help me with that or would it be better if I spoke with your manager?"

PERSON WHOSE JOB IT IS TO KEEP YOU FROM CLOSING YOUR ACCOUNT: "Your account number?"

I had a client who had horrible credit through no fault of her own (other than marrying a selfish loser). Her irresponsible ex-husband had applied for several credit cards jointly, using her Social Security number. She had been avoiding the issue for years simply because she wanted to avoid *him.* It was only when she went to purchase a home that she realized she really needed to deal with his financial wrongdoings. Clearing up her credit ended up being an opportunity to finally put an end to that unhappy chapter in her life and start afresh. Talk about a powerful metaphor.

Once the deadbeat accounts have been cleared, you can focus on your outstanding debt. It could be lots of little stuff adding up that's killing your credit. Still owe Blockbuster $20 for the movie you lost back in 1987? Write a flipping check! Didn't realize the annual membership to the gym you joined back in college was *still billing you?* Make a call and get to the bottom of it. Your entire future is on the line here.

If it is not immediately clear what is contributing to your pitiful FICO score or you just don't know what to do about your bigger balances, talk to a lender. Since this is the person who will be using that information to help determine your loan worthiness, your lender can be an invaluable resource. A particular lender's willingness and ability to help will tell you straightaway if this person is going to be a formidable force on your team (see the list of questions to ask lenders in Chapter 4 for more tips on finding a fit).

Team Up or Go Solo?

People frequently ask if I recommend finding a flipping partner. I give the same answer I would if someone asked if I recommend marriage: Wholeheartedly—as long as you choose the right teammate.

Going in on a group deal minimizes your personal risk. If you're the brawn and your dad or uncle or best friend is the brains, you've exponentially increased the skills you collectively bring to the table. Assuming your potential partner or partners have decent credit, they may also put you in a bigger league, price wise. Better still, if your crazy, rich Aunt Rita is itching to find a risky way to invest the kajillion dollars she just inherited, sign her on and open up the real estate section of your local paper.

Over the years, I have partnered with my mom several times. With her bottomless financial and emotional support and keen eye for design, she has been instrumental in my success. By alternating who holds title on a house, we can each hold a property for two years and still flip a house a year. Having two flips going simultaneously might be too much for one person, but with a partner, it allows you to minimize waste (there are *always* leftover construction materials) and maximize profits.

If you're considering a tandem jump, my best advice is to pair up with someone you know and trust implicitly. Sure, you might stumble on a potential flipping mate at a kid's birthday party (one of the parents, not the gift recipient) or on one of the Internet's many investment sites. It happens all the time, albeit with mixed results. I worked with two guys who met in cyberspace and flipped very successfully. One brought money to the table, the other brought what he thought were skills, and they actually developed a profitable working relationship. But that's definitely the exception.

After completing several winning flips with my contractor friend Darrell, he came to me with an investment opportunity. I put in $50,000, he did all the work, and we each made $100,000 in less than a year. All I had to do was put up the cash and trust him to do the right thing. It felt a bit scary at the time to just write a check, but I did it because Darrell was someone I had grown to admire and respect not just as a contractor but as a businessperson.

The bottom line: Be clear about your expectations, know what you're getting into, and get everything in writing.

Picking Your Property

If you're going to flip a house, there needs to be a house to flip. I can't say this strongly or often enough:

You make your money on the buy.

Every penny you pay for the house is one you can't spend on the renovations and carrying costs. In an appreciation-crazy market, just about any old house would have made you money if you bought it at the right price. But the biggest potential for profit lies in the house that needs a little love and is priced accordingly.

Train your eyes to see, not what is there when you're touring a home, but what *could be* there. The reason you are going to flip this house is not because you have a mad urge to wield a sledgehammer, but because there's something there you can improve. If you go in and rip everything down to bare studs, what does it take to get it all back? Money. What are you trying to make? Money. Don't throw away the very thing you're trying to make.

Your goal is to enhance, not rebuild.

Walk in the door and ask yourself:

- Does the house have some potential that's not glaringly obvious at the onset, like a tree you can clear away to double the amount of usable yard space?
- Is there an unfinished attic that would make a great in-law apartment?
- Might the house have a mountain, lake, ocean, or city skyline view if you added a second story or a deck?
- Is there a way to create four bedrooms out of three, or room to add a valuable half bath somewhere? Is there outdated wallpaper that could easily be pulled down, dreary cabinetry that's just screaming for fresh paint?
- Is there a lot line adjustment that could increase the size of the property?

Maybe your uncanny vision allows you to see that you could take away a bedroom to create a fabulous master suite with a walk-in closet and massive bathroom that will have young professionals drooling all over their Hermes ties. (This is where knowing your demographic comes in really handy.)

If the seller says, "We're not even sure where our property ends and the neighbors' begins but we think it's somewhere behind those bushes . . ." *hire a surveyor.* It will cost you a bit, but if it winds up adding major square footage to the property, you might just have found a simple way to boost your asking price.

When you spot your diamond in the rough, pay a visit to your city or county building department to find out what you can and cannot do to the property. Local zoning regulations will determine whether you can put in that pool or add that rooftop deck, and if you're counting on some addition or other to be the moneymaker on this flip, you need to know your limitations. Again, this is where your relationships can work for you. A good architect will likely have an in with the guy or gal behind the permit counter that can make or break your flip.

Location, Location, Location

It is the battle cry of Realtors everywhere, referring to the three things that matter most when finding a property. For the purposes of flipping, however, I'm going to put a bit of spin on the original idea. Initially, the mantra stressed finding a house that would appeal to the greatest number of buyers— say, in a great school district, on a quiet cul-de-sac, with a larger-than-average yard. While these things may (or may not) increase your home's final selling price (there will only be one buyer at the end of the day, and that buyer may not have kids or have any interest in gardening), certain aspects of your flip's location can put money in your pocket by virtue of sheer geographic position.

Ideally, the house you find to flip will be right in your backyard, or at least not too far away from it. In this game, time is money and if you're spending all your time commuting to the job site, *you are losing money.* You are also most familiar with the area in which you live, which will make researching and tracking the market infinitely easier.

And about that cul-de-sac. Everyone wants to live on one, right? They're quiet, there's no through traffic, families love 'em . . . but as a flipper, you might think twice before throwing down money for a house on a dead-end street. Your little end-of-the-line jewel might scream "family friendly!" but it can also mean bad parking and a tight-knit community that may not welcome you with open arms if you aren't planning to stay. How much parking is available, and how is the cement truck going to fit in there? Where is your dumpster going to sit? How noisy are the folks who live there already? Keep all this in mind when you're shopping for that gem to flip.

No one likes to think about the worst-case scenario, but successful flippers always have a Plan B. Therefore, even if your goal is to unload your renovated masterpiece in a few short weeks and never actually take possession of it, unforeseen market conditions or a sudden change in your life could throw a wrench in your plan. You may decide that even though the mortgage payments are a little steep, you *really* like the way the place turned out. You also believe in the market and in the future, and you would rather struggle with the payments than continue to throw your rent check out the virtual window. (Maybe you'll rent out that extra bedroom for a while, to help cover your costs. Way to think, smarty pants.)

Even if you currently own a home that you're perfectly happy with, what if someone were to knock on your front door and make you an offer you couldn't refuse? Or maybe once your flip is finished and you add that master suite, you'll decide to put your own house on the market instead. Could be your own home is at a price point that just happens to be selling well at the moment, or is in a great school district that you don't need any more now that your kids are grown. These are all things to consider when searching for your flip.

If you do own a house and are buying a flip, make sure your own house is in tip-top shape for sale if one of the preceding scenarios occurs. Another reason to wrap those half-finished projects at home is that you may need to draw an equity line on your own home to finish your flip—there is nothing worse than a torn-up garage or partially demolished kitchen to turn off an appraiser. Unfinished projects automatically reduce your home's value, a risk you're not in a position to take.

Some other things to take into account: Is the house you are thinking of flipping on a busy street? Is it in an area that is up-and-coming or that is still struggling to shed its shady reputation? It is one thing to get a screaming deal on a property with potential—it is another altogether to be the only sucker who didn't notice the prostitutes patrolling the street out front. Find the mangy dog on the decent block and you'll invariably strike gold.

Won't You Be My Neighbor?

If nightmare-neighbor stories were dollars, we'd all be kicking up our Gucci-clad heels in celebration. I'm not talking about the drum-banging, hedge-chopping, cop-calling guy next door here. The nasty neighbor I'm bemoaning is much, much worse. This is the man, woman, or couple on the block with nothing but time on their hands, and your cell phone number programmed into their speed dial. Perhaps your workers keep parking in front of their mailbox, or maybe they just don't like the idea of an outsider coming in and (here's that snippy tone again) flipping a house in their hood. For whatever reason, these neighbors could quickly turn into the nail in the tire of an otherwise slam-dunk flip.

Your best defense is an aggressive offense. Before the first dumpster parks out front, pay a visit to anyone you suspect might be affected by the impending construction. Apologize in advance for any noise and inconvenience they may experience, and let them know how long you expect the work to take. I have been known to invest (and believe me, it is a wise investment) in a couple dozen boxes of donuts to deliver to irritated neighbors at regular intervals. I have also baked pies and cookies and dropped them off with a note and my contact information, welcoming their comments and complaints.

When they call (and they will), muster every ounce of kindness and compassion in your body, but try to refrain from playing what I call the "neighborhood improvement card." I know from experience that this move can easily backfire. You may think that by reminding your neighbors how much you are increasing the value of the community, they will fall to their knees in gratitude. That may not be the case. The woman who has been awakened four days in a row by the sound of a jackhammer symphony essentially orchestrated by you doesn't want to hear it; neither does the man who can't afford to replace his front light fixture, much less overhaul the whole property the way you are doing with audacity and a large bankroll.

You think I'm exaggerating? I once masterminded a beautiful renovation—man, was I proud of how that house turned out—but the neighbors were in an uproar over the possible property tax hike I might have unwittingly initiated. There will always be some sour grapes on the block. Try to send them some wine before they start to whine.

Getting a Deal

I'll say it again: *You make your money on the buy.* "Well, that's fine and dandy," you say. "But isn't everyone looking to buy a dollar with fifty cents? How am I going to get my hands on the bargain-priced listings first?"

There are essentially three ways to find that unbelievable deal: (1) Use your connections, (2) make a low-price offer (inelegantly called "lowballing"), and (3) bid on a property riddled with a problem (or problems) that other buyers would find too daunting to take on. (There is a fourth way to potentially score a deal, which is to buy a house in bankruptcy or foreclosure. These can be complicated deals, but they may present an opportunity to make a nice profit. Talk to your lender if this is something you are interested in exploring.)

Connections

Let's start with your connections. Word-of-mouth can help you when you're searching for a property to flip. The key is to use discretion. If you announce to anyone who will listen that you are in the market for a fixer-upper, you could unwittingly make instant enemies with the Realtors who want to do it themselves, or with the little old lady who's in love with her house, even though she no longer needs its five bedrooms and sprawling, overgrown yard.

Still, keep your ears open. Your pharmacist may mention that her sister's neighbor was thinking about downsizing now that the kids have gone off to college—bingo! Or your banker buddy may admit that he's been thinking about selling but has so many friends who are Realtors that he is afraid of alienating or offending all of them except the one he chooses to list his place. And (drumroll, please) you're in!

Talk to friends you can trust; I find killer deals through my network all the time. Not too long ago, one of my Realtor friends called me to tell me about a client who was quietly marketing his home. The guy didn't want everyone in town to think (know) that he was broke and needed the money, so he was relying on word-of-mouth. Knowing I'm always in the market, my friend tipped me off.

The seller wanted $450,000; I offered $405,000 and he accepted. I put $30,000 into it and had an offer on the table less than three months later for $600,000—and I wasn't even finished with the renovations. While I was in escrow with this buyer, a developer approached me and explained he was buying the houses all around and behind mine. He was planning to bulldoze them all and put in a huge development. He offered me $800,000 (which I couldn't take because of the prior offer). My buyer, however, jumped on that bandwagon pronto, and made himself a nice chunk of change by doing nothing more than being in the right place at the right time.

You've Got a Lead, Now What

So, *what do you do* when you hear that a friend-of-a-friend's-friend is thinking of selling, or you spot the perfect flip that just happens not to be for sale yet? Write a letter. Explain that by selling directly to you, the homeowner can avoid the hassles of open houses and inflated Realtor fees. Announce your interest, emphasize your qualifications, but don't come right out and broadcast your intent to immediately resell. People get emotionally attached to their homes, and for good reason. If the owner raised her family there, she may feel strongly that another young family should move in and repeat her history. If the seller built the back deck with his own two hands, he may not be enchanted with your idea of bulldozing it to put in a pool.

Do not lie to your potential seller!

(You're building a relationship here, remember? Referrals are a big part of this business.) And don't fawn excessively over the property to the point where the seller begins to wonder how many other people would be dying to park their Honda in the driveway. Simply state the facts, cordially and professionally: You're interested in the house; here's what you're offering.

Your letter might sound a little like this:

Dear Mr. and Mrs. Shipwreck,

Greetings! You are receiving this letter today because I (or my spouse or partner and I) have been a secret admirer of your home for the past 15 years. Because I love your property so much, I am interested in knowing if you would consider allowing me to purchase it. I realize it is not currently on the market; however, I am prepared to make an offer that I hope will convey my capacity to facilitate a speedy and successful close of escrow.

If you would be open to selling your beautiful home, some specific components of my offer may give you the confidence to realize I can offer you what no one else can:

- No brokerage fees
- Buyer to purchase property in as-is condition with no requests for repair including Section 1 pest work
- No appraisal contingency necessary
- Seller to lease back property for 30 days at no cost

Please feel free to call me at your earliest convenience. I look forward to speaking with you!

Sincerely Yours,
J. Smartbuyer

 Toolbox

ENHANCING AN OFFER

You never know what will grab a homeowner. Here are several things that I've done to make an offer more attractive to a seller:

- A photo and personal letter may win over a sentimental seller.
- A preapproval letter from your bank showing just how well qualified you are could be your in with a financially weary seller.

- An offer to pick up the closing costs; it is a relatively small sum but a nice gesture that could put you at the front of the line.
- Arrange for a quick close—say, a 14-day escrow—and then let the seller stay for 30 days rent free to pack up at leisure.
- Try using humor. If there is a bidding war, offer an atypical price of $1,234,567 on a house that's asking $1,230,000.

Think of what you can do to strengthen your offer; then put it in writing. A caveat: Even if you are willing to provide all the preceding incentives, don't give up the farm immediately: Figure out three things you would be willing to offer and start with one or two. This leaves you some negotiating power in the likely event of a counteroffer.

Lowball Offer

The second way to score a deal is by making a low-price offer. Your best bet here is a house that has been on the market for a while with little or no activity (Realtor-speak for genuine offers). "Days on market" (DOM) is public information—simply ask the Realtor who has the listing. You can also ask if there have been any offers (maybe it just fell out of escrow or recently had a price reduction); a good Realtor can tell you the history of the property as well as the level of interest it has received (although don't be surprised if you come across a few schmucks who aren't wholly forthcoming with the facts).

Let's say a house has been on the market for 60 days at $350,000. Comps in the area (you've done this homework, remember?) are going for anywhere from $325 to $365. If it is still sitting there without a "sold" sign out front, this property is probably overpriced at $350,000. Why not write an offer at $300? "But that would insult the seller!" you cry. (You gentle, kindhearted soul, you.) Maybe. But keep in mind that selling prices are usually arrived at rather arbitrarily, and while some sellers are married to their price, others all but pick a number out of a hat, or else choose one that they would love to see materialize even though they would settle for considerably less. The power of paper is amazing; sometimes not even the sellers know what they will accept until it is in writing.

You have nothing to lose by making a reasonable, yet low-price, offer.

In theory, the sellers may feel their asking price is both fair and attainable. But "a bird in the hand" (in this case, your written, sincere offer) could be enough to change their mind. The seller can and probably will make a counteroffer, so if in the preceding example, $300,000 is the absolute max you would be willing to pay, consider writing your original offer for even less, say $285,000. This leaves you some haggle room—and if you're really lucky, the seller might just take it without a fight. This is where having experienced professionals on your team can pay off. Ask your Realtor to discuss with the seller's Realtor why your offer is fair (by pulling up similarly priced comps or pointing out the property's flaws and drawbacks).

The low-bid strategy has paid off for me countless times. Just recently, my housekeeper Teresa purchased her first home. She didn't ask me for money; she came to me and said

41

that she and her husband, a painter, had managed to save $14,000 and wanted to buy a house. I was torn. In the little slice of overpriced heaven we call home, $14,000 couldn't get you in the front door of even the most dilapidated structure in town, and Teresa had absolutely no credit, so 100 percent financing was not an option. On the other hand, I felt strongly that if she had managed to squirrel away such a significant sum, she deserved to own a house. I assured her I would help her and we set about on our search.

Following my own advice, we found a property in Teresa's neighborhood, a nice little fixer-upper with a history of bad additions and even worse tenants. It had been on the market for around two months at $589,000. (Remember, this is Santa Barbara.) We wrote an offer for $485,000—*more than a hundred thousand dollars less than the asking price*—and got it. (In fact, we even negotiated a thousand-dollar credit during our final walk-through three days prior to closing escrow, because the tenants had left the place in worse condition than when we wrote the offer.) All in all, proof once again that sometimes even sellers don't know what they will accept until it is in writing.

After we closed, I loaned Teresa $100,000 and my free design expertise and we set about fixing up the place, including finishing off a separate back unit that she planned to rent out to help cover the mortgage. With the help of the team of construction experts I have assembled over the years, we completed the renovations in just four weeks. Now all we had to do was refinance. The new bank appraisal came in at $800,000, leaving Teresa with over $200,000 in equity (after she paid me back, of course).

My willingness to make an "insulting" offer, coupled with the strong relationship I have with my lender (who granted

Teresa and me a joint loan, helping her build credit from the get-go), resulted in the ultimate win-win. After six months of on-time mortgage payments, the loan was transferred entirely into Teresa's name.

No, I didn't make a penny off of Teresa's deal, but because of the many houses I'd flipped before hers, I was in a position (both financially and experientially) to help someone I care deeply about change the course of her life. I consider that one hell of a payoff.

 Toolbox

USING AN ASSIGNEE

Always put in contracts the right to transfer the existing deal to another party should you elect to. It is a simple matter of adding "or assignee" each time there is a blank for the buyer's name. Doing this gives you a potential out during escrow if for some reason you cannot or do not wish to close the deal. The assignee then can keep the same terms you initially agreed to and secured with your contract.

Unwanted Property

The third way you can make money on the buy is by finding a property with so many red flags that you can hardly see the place for all the dust around it (kicked up by potential buyers running away from it at warp speed). This approach is not for the faint of heart, nor is it necessarily the best choice for first timers.

At any given time, there is likely to be a lemon on the market in your neighborhood and price range. In the real estate world, word spreads faster than colds in a kindergarten classroom. Ask your Realtor about properties considered to be pariahs. Maybe there is a nifty little three-bedroom with a cracked foundation with your name on it right around the corner. Perhaps some nasty mold was recently discovered behind the bedroom wall of your future flip. Some guy didn't pull any permits before he added a master bath? Get your butt over there, pronto.

Just because other buyers are scared away doesn't mean you should be, too. With some due diligence (and maybe just a pinch of insanity, to be honest), the less-than-perfect house can turn into the perfect flip. If a faulty foundation is turning people away, do some research. You might discover you can fix it for a couple thousand dollars. If you can buy it for $4,000 less than the next guy, you have already made two grand.

This is where getting multiple bids for a job can pay off. You always want to submit the highest bid when requesting a credit, even though you may go with a lesser one (or choose to do the work yourself, if you're qualified).

I once scored a house for a song when I learned that the house needed $15,000 in termite repairs. Knowing that normally it is the seller's obligation to repair visible termite damage, I wrote my offer accordingly and waived his obligation to do the work. I knew I would be demolishing a lot of what was termite infested, so it wasn't a huge deal to me. He got what he wanted (a quick sale), and I got what I wanted (a dump for a song). It was a clear-cut win-win.

Keep in mind that just by writing an offer, you're not obligated to buy the house. Unearth something deal breaking during your inspections and all you have lost is the cost of the inspection, invariably money well spent. You may have actually created an opportunity to renegotiate the price if you discover a flaw that would turn off the average buyer. Just be certain when you write your offer that you're not dismissing important contingencies in an effort to make your offer more attractive. Contingencies are there to protect you and your deposit, so take advantage of every last one.

If the property you're considering has a few problems, this is not the time to request or settle for a rush escrow. Give yourself plenty of time to get the place thoroughly inspected and compile estimates for any work that needs to be done. Go the extra mile, get the extra survey, use the notoriously expensive but nitpicky guy. Once you have completed your inspections and know that it is going to cost $X to replace the war-torn roof or $Y to reinforce the illegally added second story, you may even get your seller to kick back a nice little credit through escrow. The more painstakingly you prepare now, the less likely you will be hit over the head with the anvil of despair after you have closed, and discover your house needs thousands of dollars of work you didn't factor into your accounting.

A long escrow can pay off in other ways as well. Planning and measuring spaces and ordering materials takes time: Why not do most of it during the period (escrow) when you have no carrying costs (mortgage, property tax, etc.)? You will want to wait to spend any money until after the point during the proceedings at which you have released all your contingencies. But once the deal is a "sure thing" (so to speak, because we both know there's no such thing in reality), I have no problem putting down payments on big-ticket items that require lengthy lead times. Each decision set in stone frees you up to move ahead and tackle the next one. You cannot imagine the sheer number of decisions you will have made by the time this whole experience is a memory. The more you do up front, the less you are going to have to do later when you are overwhelmed and exhausted.

 Toolbox

WORK BEFORE ESCROW CLOSES?

Ask your seller if you can start your work or move some things in before escrow technically closes. A good Realtor representing your seller won't agree in a million years (for liability reasons), but you never know. You could save money when buying fixtures at closeout or furniture to use for staging by taking it off the floor of the showroom immediately and having it delivered right away.

Chapter Summary

1. **Determine your goals, needs, profit requirements, and risk profile.** What would it take for you to feel your flip was successful? Would breaking even or losing money be the end of the world? The answers to these questions may not mean much to you now, but it is important to search your soul early on. Once you find your property and crunch some numbers, you will need to know where you stand emotionally and financially.

2. **Become a real estate market expert.** Start going to every open house you can squeeze into your schedule. Talk to real estate agents, bankers, people you know who have bought and sold properties, anyone with any connection to the business. Start a file and collect names and information. The more you're "out there," the more quickly you will spot a great deal and snag it.

3. **Clean up your credit.** How fiscally responsible you have been in the past will directly influence how much you can borrow and how cheaply you can borrow it (your interest rate). Before you find that perfect property, reconciling outstanding debts or establishing credit if you have none at all, will save you a great deal of heartache.

4. **Decide if you can swing it solo or need a partner.** Partners minimize financial risk and may bring some skills to the job, but they also can complicate a flip. Carefully weigh all the pros and cons associated with your potential partner or partners before joining forces. If you team up, get everything in writing.

5. **Start your search.** I can't say it enough: You make your money on the buy. Be painstaking in your search for the right house at the right price. When you alone can see the vision or can get the house for less than anyone else—even if it is because you were so bold as to write an unsolicited letter to the owner of a home not yet for sale—you are already leaps and bounds ahead of the competition.

4

ASSEMBLING YOUR TEAM

Flip·ping point (ˊflip-iŋ pöint) *n.*   The moment (usually early in a flip) when you recognize and admit your weaknesses and fill in with professionals where needed.

As multitalented as I am sure you are, my guess is that you're not a Realtor *and* a contractor *and* an architect *and* a designer *and* an accountant *and* completely out of your mind. Therefore, you're going to need to bring in some hired guns to help you do this deal. But first, you should determine what you bring to the table.

At the age of 23 when I bought my first property, I had no idea I was going to become a flipper. It took some time and several houses to figure out what my unique gifts are, and perhaps more important, what they aren't. On one project, I came to the conclusion that backbreaking, manual labor (digging 18-inch deep trenches for wall footings) wasn't my natural talent. On another house, it occurred to me that complex accounting (tracking expenses on a spreadsheet with my self-taught Excel skills) ranks just behind root canal surgery on my personal fun scale. Eventually, it became clear that my design experience and aptitude gave me an edge in that corner, and that my love of real estate—coupled with the license I eventually obtained—was another bonus. For every house I flip, those are the two hats I wear and therefore two items I can shave off the budget right from the start.

On smaller jobs, I also crown myself Project Manager and run my own crew. But by now I know my strengths, and when the scope of a remodel requires a plethora of permits, complex engineering, or major changes to the house, I hire a general contractor.

Maybe your contribution is clear (your day job or hobby relates directly to buying, renovating, or selling houses), but then again maybe it's not. The truth is, you may not realize what your flipping forte will be until you've gone through the process. You may pride yourself on your reputation as a number-crunching phenomenon, but in the throes of remodeling when receipts are flying at you like balls in a batting cage and bills are forming a formidable paper fence right there on your desk, you may suddenly and inexplicably change your tune.

Getting down and dirty in the trenches—I mean literally, when the laborers don't show up to dig the ditch that needs to be dug before the electrician comes tomorrow and it's raining—is an inevitable and invaluable part of this business. Be prepared to do it. You may just discover that stripping old, buried beams of a hundred years' worth of paint is quite your cup of tea. Cha-ching! That is one less guy you've got to hire.

Let's say that after a long, painful self-inspection, you conclude that you don't have a single skill to bring to the table that will directly impact your bottom line. Don't despair. Surely you know at least one person on the planet who'd be willing to pitch in. (If you have an uncanny ability to get people to do things for free, flipping is definitely for you.) Maybe you have a friend who works at an appliance warehouse and can score you a discount, or your sister-in-law is a lender and can waive your closing costs. Hey, even your "between-jobs" buddy—the one who might be convinced to come to your painting party in exchange for a few tall boys—counts here. A warm body willing and able to work is much better than nothing.

The point is, any little connection or "in" (and that includes the aforementioned gratis grunt work) you can exploit puts you ahead of the game, which can really set the tone for the flip. Sometimes I joke that I should have married a contractor and had an affair with a lender, but all kidding aside, the more people you have in your court at tip-off time, the more money you'll have in your pocket when you turn over the keys to your buyer.

Speaking of significant others . . . if you have a spouse or partner who has something practical to contribute to your new career, consider it an extraordinary gift. But the undying, unyielding support of your significant other should be non-negotiable. Anyone who's married to a golfer knows the term *golf widow* all too well. There are also work widows, workout widows, window-washing widows, the list goes on and on. Flipping houses may not be the first or last time-suck your relationship endures, but it'll be a significant one. If your partner isn't willing to (temporarily) lose you to your new love, the emotional strain can ruin your relationship *and* your flip.

51

This chapter outlines the other players you need on your team as well as how to find, manage, and profit from each. I beg you: Don't just scan over the headings and declare, "Hrmph! I can do *that* myself." I'm sure you can. With time and proper instruction, I'll bet you could also design nuclear warheads, pilot a rocket, and perform arthroscopic surgery on your own knee. But if you were doing all those things, chances are you wouldn't be doing any of them well.

One of the secrets of successful flipping is

Know your limitations.

If it's going to take you three weeks to sand a floor that's going to look like your second grader did it when all is said and done, hire a professional. If you don't have a good sense of space but your Realtor and several friends feel that the floor plan needs to be reconfigured, fork over for a professional architect. If you were absent the day they were handing out an aptitude for color and finishes, find yourself an interior designer with good taste. (They may seem like expenses you don't want to incur, but in the end they will save you time and money and you'll end up with a much more saleable result.)

Your Agent

I promise I'm not going to suggest you master every skill required by your team, but in all honesty, the best way to find a real estate agent you can trust to stay on top of the market is to become one yourself. This allows you to save tons of money in fees and also keeps you in the market's inner loop, where information on the best houses sometimes never leaves.

If your desire to flip houses genuinely comes from an interest in the industry, it may indeed be time to take it to the next level and get your license. However, a real estate license should not be taken lightly. It is a tremendous responsibility that carries a great liability risk. As an agent, you can be held legally responsible for everything from stating false square footage (you mean, you can't guesstimate?) to not disclosing the moldy plank the buyer found in the basement (you didn't even know the piece of wood was there). Become an agent because you want to be on top of the game—but take your profession seriously once you're there. It is a serious business and in every transaction, hundreds of thousands of dollars may be at stake.

If you *do* decide to become an agent, use your license when you buy, but still consider hiring an unbiased associate when you sell. I have found it is much better to have someone else list a property once there's an emotional attachment.

When I first got interested in real estate, I'd go to open houses because I enjoyed looking at beautiful homes. I realized I was a bona fide flipper when I got more excited about seeing dumps. Every ad that announced "handyman special" or "lots of potential" had me salivating. Eventually I got to the point where I couldn't resist sneaking a peek inside any house on the market, from the condemned mold factory to the most grandiose mansion. Both instilled in me inspiration and delight. If spending your Sunday mornings on caravan with your cup of Starbucks in hand doesn't delight you, you'll need to work with someone who already has that spark.

In fact, if every aspect of the industry—from inventory to interest rates to which hovels are selling at what price—doesn't stir up your curiosity, or your other career and family already occupy 103 percent of your time, don't waste your time and energy vying for a real estate license. You can still flip successfully, but you are going to have to rely on an excellent agent and be willing to develop and nurture that relationship.

Having outside help is for you if you don't have time to market and show your property, or to follow up with potential buyers. An unbiased party also helps you avoid the common pitfall of becoming too emotionally attached to your property to price it aggressively and get it sold.

When searching for your property pro, look for someone who is an expert in your area and who shares your goals and philosophy. Finding the right agent is like finding your soul mate: You trust the agent implicitly to do the right thing for you and your flipping career, and the agent in turn is eternally grateful for your business and loyalty. If you were dating, there would be a neon "get a room!" sign over your heads. That's the kind of lovefest I'm talking about here.

Famously fickle? Get over it. I'm a big advocate of establishing a loyal, long-term relationship with your agent as she can really be your ace in the hole, whether by finding undiscovered gems for you or closing otherwise impossible deals. I still refer friends to the agent my parents used when they bought their first home in Pacific Palisades in 1983. That being said, if you question your real estate agent's professionalism, availability, or dedication, discuss it or move on. There are plenty of fish in this sea, and you should never settle for a mediocre agent.

The best way to meet and greet agents is by going to open houses. Some will be cordial and laid back; others will attack you like a rabid dog. It's really a matter of personal preference, but keep in mind that while Cujo may be a bit off-putting, he probably has a packed Rolodex. To me, the ideal is someone who is assertive without being aggressive.

When you see those sparks, ask if you can set up an informational interview. Following is a list of suggested questions you might ask, along with the answers you're looking for:

- **How long have you been in the business?** Since the average family moves every five to six years, ideally your Realtor will have six or more years of experience (and thus is starting to see some repeat business).
- **Are you an expert in this neighborhood?** You need someone who "gets" your hood and can sell it to potential buyers. Can she give you an off-the-cuff list of every church/school/dog park/walking trail/Starbucks in a two-mile radius? If not, move on.
- **What do you charge for your commission and is it negotiable?** Six percent is the industry standard, so you probably want someone whose commission is half of that, right? Wrong! Money motivates people. The bigger percentage of the sale price she is working for, the more motivated your Realtor will be to sell your pad for top dollar. Once you've flipped a few houses and have gotten addicted to the process (and the payoff), it's perfectly reasonable to discuss a possible reduced commission rate for the staggering volume of repeat business you'll be sending her way.
- **What kind of advertising and marketing do you provide for your clients?** A good agent will have a list of marketing tools available: flyers, a web site, print advertisements, newsletters, community information worksheets, photo tours, and so on. The best way to sell your home is by having an agent who knows how to

price it right, get it in escrow quickly and painlessly, and most important, get it closed. So yes, peruse the portfolio—but ask the hard questions (such as, how many successful closings do you manage a year?), too.

- **Are you available via cell phone or e-mail?** When time is money, both of these forms of communication are critical. Ask how often she checks e-mail and how early or late you can call. Getting in touch with the agent during *your* most convenient times may be important to you.

- **Do you work on weekends?** This isn't about balance—this is about hiring the person who will get the most exposure for your house at the time when most buyers are out there looking. If her standing Saturday golf game is nonnegotiable (and she doesn't have a partner or assistant who is available 24/7 or doesn't make you feel confident that another agent in the office will gladly hold open houses for you every weekend) find another Realtor.

- **How do you balance work with your outside or family obligations?** Again, this is a business. First timers often require lots of handholding, and you want to be sure your real estate agent has a few free digits to grab onto when you're feeling needy.

- **Do you use a lockbox?** A lockbox is a handy tool because any Realtor with a universal key can get into the house and show the property. Since your property will likely be vacant, a lockbox should pose little risk if your Realtor offers this disclaimer: "Yes, I have a lockbox I'd like to use to make showing your house easier. I understand that you might be worried about theft or abuse of your property, which is why I will diligently check the box daily and personally follow up with every agent who shows your home."

- **Do you have an assistant?** An agent with a high volume of transactions probably has an assistant. If that's the case, the answer you want to hear is, "Yes, his name is Sam, and he will be contacting you every other day during the course of our escrow to see if you have any doubts, questions, or concerns." A licensed assistant can also hold open houses in the event your Realtor is otherwise engaged. (Of course, any licensed agent can hold an open house, but one who has been involved from the get-go will be better prepared to answer potential buyers' questions.)

- **Do you have a strong relationship with a particular title or escrow company?** Agents who respond to this question with a resounding "Yes!" may be able to score you some free perks by virtue of their copious business dealings. They might also negotiate a binder on your insurance policy that saves you money when you go to sell. Sometimes, however, the choice of title or escrow companies won't be yours (or your Realtor's), so the stronger connections she has, the better.

YOUR ATTORNEY

You should always have the name and number of a trusty real estate lawyer programmed into your speed dial. Ask your agent or lender for referrals and make an introductory phone call. Don't wait until a problem arises to initiate this relationship.

Your Lender

It goes without saying that the person with the ability to grant or deny access to massive amounts of cash is a critical player on your team. Here again is where your relationships can pay off.

If you have never bought anything more substantial than a winter coat, it is time to hit the pavement. To be a star flipper, you need a friendly lender in your back pocket. Local banks are your best bet, as sellers frequently frown on offers from an out-of-town institution. That is not to say that you'll never close a deal if you choose your sister-in-law in Hawaii as your financier. However, if yours is one of multiple offers, you want to do everything you can to make it as attractive as possible.

A quick word about money: A lender will take several factors into account (primarily your income, credit score, and the price and value of the property in question) to determine how much money you are eligible to borrow.

Nowhere is it stated that
you have to borrow it all.

Since lenders are in the business of making money, the more you borrow, the more they make. Remember, borrowed money is not free money. You will be paying mortgage payments and costly interest on it (depending on the length of time you wind up borrowing it). Only you can determine your borrowing comfort zone.

Start at the bank where you do most or all of your personal banking and set up an appointment with a loan officer. (If you insist on keeping all your cash in a sock in the freezer, ask friends for referrals.) Explain your intentions—that you're buying to flip and that if all goes well, you hope to do it again. You will not appreciate the true value of having a solid relationship with a personal banker until you need last-minute funds wired into your account to go toward your down payment and it's the Friday before a holiday. A loyal banker will find a way to make it happen.

Following is a list of questions to ask potential lenders, along with the answers you're looking for:

- **Is there any benefit to having an existing checking or savings account here, or to opening one before I apply for a loan?** There should be some sort of incentive for banking with a lender that gets your loan business, such as a lower interest rate (up to half of a point, which ain't chump change), faster fund transfers, or no fees for Internet access. Ask and you very well may receive.

- **How quickly can I get a preapproval letter?** Please note the distinction between a prequalification letter and a preapproval letter. With the former, you have met with your lender and he has, based on information you provided verbally, said in essence, "This institution is probably going to be lending this person money." The information you have given, however, has not been reviewed or approved by an underwriter (the actual money source), so it's a preliminary step. Better than nothing, certainly, as it shows you have not been flat-out rejected. Much stronger is the preapproval letter, which says "We have gone through this borrower's financial underwear drawer and will be granting him $X, subject to an appraisal of the property in question." When you're actively searching for properties, you want that preapproval letter available to you at a moment's notice.

- **Where should my credit score be to take advantage of your best programs?** Although this will vary from lender to lender, it always pays to know where you stand going in. Your potential lender may scan over your credit report and see that you're on the brink of significant savings by just paying off one card or selling that car you're paying through the nose for (and may not even be in love with). The answer you want here is, "Let's take a look at your report and see what we can do." A flat numerical answer tells you he's not all that interested in helping your cause.

- **What sort of junk fees can you waive**? There are lots of things you may be charged for that are either inflated or flat-out fluff—hence the categorical tag. Things like "document prep," "underwriting," and "processing" or "service" fees are all costs a lender may be willing to waive. Simply by asking the question, you're showing that you are aware of such goings-on.

- **If I set up an automatic withdrawal of my mortgage payment from my bank account can I save some money in points or fees?** If there is a bank affiliated with your lender, this should be an option you can take advantage of. I've saved ¼ of a percent in interest, which can add up nicely. It really depends on how cheap money is at any given moment, and how much of it they're lending out, but it certainly can't hurt to ask.

- **How much do you charge for an appraisal?** Prices for appraisals can vary greatly, but if a lender quotes you a figure greater than $1,000, ask if there are any alternative options.

- **How soon after closing can I establish an equity line of credit?** If you're putting less than 20 percent of the purchase price down, you may have to do some visible improvements and get the property reappraised before your lender will be willing to dish out any more money. Nevertheless, you need to be sure that cash will be forthcoming if and when you need it. If you're putting 20 percent or more down, you should be able to get an equity line shortly after you close.
- **Do you communicate via e-mail?** Wasted time means wasted money, so you want to get all your documents as quickly as humanly (or electronically) possible. Nothing tests your patience like a procrastinating or inaccessible lender holding up your closing on a flip when you're prepped and ready to start work.
- **What is the best way to reach you on weekends?** Many times, I have stumbled on the perfect flip at an open house on a Sunday and needed a preapproval letter to make that superstrong offer that very day. Don't stop pestering until you have a BlackBerry address, a contact at the gym who can track him down on the treadmill, and the cell phone number of the dog walker for his kids' nanny's poodle.

Once you settle on a lender, you can get into your financing options. All other things being equal, the lowest interest rates typically are granted when you need to borrow 80 percent or less of the purchase price. If you have less than 20 percent to put down, or nothing at all, you'll need to borrow a greater portion of the purchase price. It is still fine and doable; you'll just pay a higher interest rate.

Back when I first started flipping, I was the poster girl for the 30-year-fixed loan. They're the blue-chip stocks of the banking world: They're the safe, long-term standby. Your parents probably had one, may have even paid it off a year or two early. Call me Gomer Pyle, but I didn't even know there were other options. Learn from my stupidity. Even when your lender's interest rates are shockingly low, if you know you're going to be selling a house shortly, 30-year-fixed is not the way to go. Think about it: You're paying for the privilege of having that great rate for *30 years* (which, God willing and unless you're a truly ham-fisted flipper, is not going to happen). In the short time that you'll carry the loan, you won't pay off any of the principal because fixed loans have all of the interest front-loaded anyway.

Your goal is to spend the least amount of money during the flipping process so you wind up with the most in your pocket at the end of it. With all due respect to my dear departed dad, "creative financing" is no longer the scary, rogue move it once was; it's the name of the flipping game.

Let's say you think you can finish all the work that needs to be done and have the house back on the market in two months. You may opt for an interest-free or even negative amortization loan (where you pay only a portion of the interest and the remaining portion gets tacked onto the principal, or balance, that you'll pay off when you sell). Maybe there's a promotional program where you won't have to make your first payment for two months after you close. A lender who knows your goals and plans can set you up with the right loan.

Whatever you do, make sure there are no prepayment penalties associated with your loan. I once had a client whose escrow was scheduled to close the day before the long New Year's weekend. She was already selling the property at a loss because she had taken out equity loans she couldn't repay. One day before the closing, she got a call from her banker informing her she had a $16,000 prepayment penalty. Now, as her Realtor, I had asked her the two questions I always ask: Did you own the property for at least two years ("Yes"), and do you have a prepayment penalty on your loan ("No"). Technically, it was the lender's fault we weren't made aware of this fact earlier (although my client should have known this all along), but the point was moot. She was obligated to sell the house and pay the penalty. The moral of this story: Ask questions. Demand clarification. Be tenacious. The more you know, the better off you are.

Market conditions change, and loans vary from lender to lender, but here are a few types that may be available:

- **Monthly Option Adjustable Rate Mortgages (ARMs).** These loans will have payments based on an initial interest rate from 1.0 percent to 5.0 percent. The interest rate will adjust monthly. This is calculated by adding a margin to a particular index. The most widely used index today is the Month Treasury Average Index (MTA; 12-month average of the one-year T-bill). These loans are great for investors who want the lowest payment while they are fixing up a property and then selling it. However, the way these loans are now being priced by lenders, they are at or higher than a 5/1 interest only loan when they adjust. The reason for this is that the secondary market does not want to purchase most of these loans because they are candidates to be refinanced or sold.

- **Fixed Loans for 5/1, 7/1, or 10/1 years.** These loans are fixed for an initial period of time and interest only payment then will adjust once a year with a margin between 2.25 to 2.75 over the LIBOR (London Interbank Offered Rate or one-year T-bill). In today's market, I would probably recommend a 5/1 ARM for investors who are flipping as it gives them the time they need and the rate will be lower than the monthly option ARM. If they are holding an investment property, the 10/1 ARM provides a rate at .375 to .50 percent less than the 30-year fixed.

- **30-Year Fixed Mortgage.** A bank offers these fully amortized with a fixed payment that allows you to pay off the loan within the specified time period and with interest only. If the investors want to keep the property, are not considering selling it, and feel rates will be increasing, then this is the product for them. Also, lenders have come out with a 40-year amortization on a fixed rate that could revolutionize the way we buy real estate and increase our borrowing potential.

Lenders now have the ability to lend to limited liability companies (LLCs) at the same pricing on the loans as on a title held by an individual. Lenders may also offer a *stated asset stated income* 75 percent first loan to $650,000 with a combined loan to value up to 75 percent and can lend up to $1,000,000 first loan at 70 percent loan to value with a 25 percent combined loan to value. Also, on Verification Assets a lender may be able to go to $2,000,000 with a $1,000,000 line of credit behind it to a 75 percent loan to value.

There are lots of online sites where you can research financing options before you go to the bank: www.loanpage .com is one example.

Your Contractor

On the one hand, sweat equity is a great way to get and stay ahead financially, so if you're skilled in the building arts and know your way around a toolshed, by all means dust off your hard hat and get out there. On the other hand, if you don't know a band saw from a belt sander, this is not the time to be cavalier about essential skills.

A general contractor gets paid to oversee the job, from hiring and managing the subcontractors (electricians, plumbers, finish carpenters, etc.) to securing permits and ordering materials. If it's a large construction company, he may have one or more foremen working under him managing the details of each job. In the early days, I remember being so excited to see huge crews working on my jobs—until payday rolled around. The bottom line is the more tasks you're willing to tackle yourself, the fatter your wallet will stay.

For first-time flippers, I recommend starting with a small cosmetic fixer you can manage yourself. This forces you to be in charge and present on your job site daily, you know exactly who is getting paid what, and you're not paying a markup on every last material and service. Doing a minimally invasive fix your first time around also allows you to test your creative skills in terms of fixtures, flooring, hardware, and paint.

Alas, if you don't have the time, skills, or inclination to be personally involved in the renovations, you'll need to hire someone who does. That person and his subcontractors ("subs") will make up your crew. They will be an integral part of the whole experience and will directly contribute to the success or failure of your flip.

When assembling your crew, referrals are your first line of offense. When Bob knows you hired him because of the great job he did on your sister Brenda's house, it boosts your trust in him and his sense of accountability to you. Ask everyone you meet or see—your real estate agent, lender, hairdresser, tennis partner, chiropractor, yoga instructor, dry cleaner, and masseuse—if they have used or know of a reputable contractor. Eventually you'll strike gold and accumulate at least three names.

Now it's time to set up some interviews. Following is a list of suggested questions, along with the answers you're looking for:

- **So-and-so referred me to you. Please tell me honestly how it was working with him/her.** This is an opportunity for the contractor to tell you that he really appreciated that your friend paid him on time, was clear with direction, and was a good decision maker—or not. Listen closely when the contractor answers this question: Does he dodge it or answer it easily? Communication is key if this relationship is going to be successful. You don't want the guy who just says what you want to hear; you want the one who can be forthright even when the subject is touchy.
- **How many of your projects have come in on time and on budget?** "Most if not all," would be ideal in theory, but the reality is that most projects do not come in on time or at or under budget. That's just the nature

of this game. This question, however, tests his honesty and opens the door to the next question.

- **How do you handle change orders?** Change orders refer to any decisions, additions, and changes that deviate from the original plan or budget. The *only* answer you want to hear here is, "I go over any costs you will incur as a result of requested changes prior to executing them. You will have a clear idea of how any change will affect your budget and time line before we prep/build/rip it out, and you will have it in writing before we execute the change."

- **I'd like to start in three weeks. Does that suit your schedule, and how much time on a daily basis can you dedicate to my project?** You may be hoping desperately that he'll say, "I've got all the time in the world for you!" Unfortunately, that's either not an honest answer, or he's not the best in the business (if he was, would his dance card be completely empty?). A reputable, experienced pro will have other clients, and you deserve to know how many and how likely your job is to get bumped for one with seniority.

- **How long have you been in business?** The new guy eager to beef up his resume may offer you the screaming deal of a lifetime, but a well-seasoned veteran with a team of reliable subs in place is probably a better choice. Look for someone with a minimum of five years of experience with local tradespeople.

- **How's your relationship with the folks who give out the building permits?** In Fantasy Construction Land: "I pull permits on a weekly basis and know the politics of the counter and the personal story of everyone behind it. What's more, I am familiar with the system for permits that won't be issued for a long time and for over-the-counter permits I can get right away. I know my way around the city and county permitting offices, and I have never had a permit held up because my application wasn't complete."

- **How often do you bill and what is your markup?** This will vary depending on where you live, but anything in the 10 to 24 percent range is a standard markup in the industry. Some contractors bill weekly, others monthly. Determine what payment schedule will work best for your financial situation (maybe paying monthly will allow you to hold onto your cash longer and not pay equity line interest) and see if he is willing to accommodate it.

- **How many foremen work for you? Can you tell me a bit about the one who will be managing my job?** Your hope should be that he doesn't manage more than four or five foremen—or he may be too busy to give you the time of day. The best answer to the latter half of the question would go something along these lines: "One of my most reliable and experienced superintendents is going to be available for your project. He understands the time-sensitive nature of your job and excels at managing crews efficiently." Casually ask if all your questions and concerns will go through the foreman, or if you can contact the contractor directly. In some big construction companies, the contractor is more of a figurehead than a working member of the team. The superintendent may be your separated-at-birth soul sister and you might actually prefer working with her. Either way, it's good to know what you're getting before you sign on any dotted lines.

- **Would you be interested in some kind of profit-sharing or incentive for finishing early?** It may sound cynical, but with less-than-scrupulous types, financial incentives may inspire sloppy work rather than the cocktail of excellence and efficiency you bellied up to the bar for. Unless you plan to partner up with this guy, save this question for later. But, if you know the contractor well, trust him implicitly, and are intimately familiar with the quality of his work, this may be something you want to throw out there. With the right person, incentives such as these can help you stay on budget and within your time line.

- **Do you always pick up your cell phone during business hours? Do you communicate via e-mail?** You're probing his accessibility; I always like to ask this question because it makes me look like I know that there will be questions and that I expect to get answers. E-mail is not only a great way to communicate, but also provides a handy documentation of events if an unforeseen conflict should arise.

- **Do you have a web site?** A legitimate contactor interested in growing his business should have a web site. Peruse it for his bio, photos of his work, and testimonials from former clients.

- **Could I look at some of your finished projects to examine the quality of your work?** An immediate and enthusiastic "You betcha!" should be forthcoming. A contractor with something to hide or a bad reputation will give you lies and excuses, not names and addresses.

- **If you give me a bid for my scope of work and the bill I receive is radically different, how will you**

69

handle the difference? Most contractors charge for a combination of time and materials. There is no right answer to this question; you're asking it to make him aware that you know there can be a discrepancy between these two numbers and that although you know unforeseen costs can arise, you expect him to work with you to come up with a figure that is fair.

- **Have you ever placed a lien on a client's property**? A lien is basically the right to take, hold, or sell property when due payment isn't forthcoming. If a contractor doesn't get paid for the work he did, he can legally make a claim on the property. You're hoping your contractor hasn't had to go down this road, but chances are if he has, it was his deadbeat client's fault, not his own, so don't panic if he says yes. It's not like finding out your cardiac surgeon has been involved in 13 wrongful death lawsuits. If your contractor *has* had to place a lien, view it as an opportunity to peer into his psyche. Ask him how he handled the situation. His answer will tell you more about his character and ethics than any resume ever could.

- **Are you licensed and insured?** In California where I live, anyone who contracts for a job valued at more than $500 (labor and materials) must have a current, valid license from the Contractors State License Board. Licensed contractors are required to carry liability and workers' compensation insurance—their unlicensed competitors are not. Check http://contractors-license.org to see if the guy you're considering is licensed in your state.

- **How do you feel about letting me pay directly for big-ticket items such as cabinets or appliances?**

I've saved some money shopping for items like this on my own in the past, but trying to shave costs here can burn you, too. If you pay for some materials directly, your contractor may not be willing to coordinate their installation and delivery. Also, if something goes wrong, *you alone* are responsible. If your contractor's electrician and plumber are prepping the kitchen for cabinets, the easiest move may be to let the contractor order them, too. But if he tells you it's fine for you to be involved, you can assume he respects your budget mindedness and won't try to undermine it at every turn.

- **If I pay you in cash can I get a better deal?** All-cash transactions can make keeping track of expenses and payments tricky—but it's worth asking if it can significantly boost your bottom line. Just know that you will need to be meticulous about itemizing and tracking your receipts. Which brings us to . . .

- **Will I get copies of all receipts?** When you go to sell your recently improved residence, you'll be taxed on any profit you make. Therefore, you want every shred of evidence showing precisely what it cost you to buy, carry, improve, and sell the property. You don't just want to *see* all your receipts, you want to save and review them to make sure there are no accounting errors.

- **Have you worked on this particular style of house?** The guy who's had extensive experience redesigning Tudors, farmhouses, or bungalows similar to yours can be an invaluable (read: free) design resource. Did houses of your era have crown molding or cove ceilings or mosaic tile floors? An experienced renovator may

71

save you time and money by virtue of his comprehensive knowledge.

- **What do you think is your best attribute?** "I am best known for my honesty and integrity," is what you'd like to hear, but any answers involving the words honesty, punctuality, integrity, or organization (and not involving the words "parole officer") are good signs.

Let's say Larry passed your little test with flying colors. Before you officially hire him, ask yourself: Is he punctual, reliable, and equipped with a magnificent sense of humor? Do you *like* him? Like spending time with him? Your crew has a huge impact on what I like to call the *spirit* of the job. You need folks who can roll with the inevitable punches. Things will go wrong. Plumbing will back up, mold will be found, materials will be misplaced and misordered. All these things are right up there with death and taxes on the list of Life's Little Inevitabilities. You want an easygoing, likeminded crew on board to help solve whatever issues arise, and perhaps have a laugh or two along the way. If the bricks lining your new front walkway seem downright charismatic compared with the guy you hired to put them in, you're in for a long, lonely ride.

After you have established your crew and successfully completed a project or two with them, you may want to discuss monetary incentives for them to finish more quickly and share in a piece of the profits. Keep this in mind when you are first assembling your crew: Could you go into business with these people? Are they willing to be a part of your team and work side by side with you to get the job done in a timely, professional manner?

I'm a big fan of pep talks. I like to tell my crew every morning that I am grateful to them for being there. I remind them that because we have a common goal (to go home at the end of the day with all our fingers still attached), safety comes first, with speed and efficiency close behind.

Remember the old joke, "Your looks and a quarter will buy you a phone call"? (This was back when the quarter could still buy a phone call.) Well, one of my pep talks and a big box of donuts go a long way. A few dozen Krispy Kremes are a great way to get your team fired up on a Monday morning. Homemade cookies can get them over the Wednesday hump. And nothing says, "I think you're swell" like dropping off free lunch on Fridays. These are little things you can do to show the cogs in your flipping wheel just how important they are to you.

Here's another tip: Before I unveil my finished pad at the first open house, I like to invite anyone who contributed in any small way to a little completion party. Subcontractors that I used early on in the project might otherwise never get to see the final result. Plus, a party is a nice way to enjoy the final project together and also see how it handles a large gathering. When the toilet overflows or I discover the dishwasher was never hooked up, it gives me one last opportunity to get the bugs out.

COMPETITIVE BIDS

For every job you do, you should always get at least three comparable bids. Even after you've settled in with a crew that is trustworthy and compatible, it's

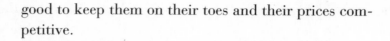

good to keep them on their toes and their prices competitive.

Chapter Summary

1. **Determine what you bring to the table.** Your skills, connections, and knowledge will directly impact your bottom line. At the same time, it is essential to know your limitations. If the work you did would be substandard, bring in professional help.

2. **Find a fabulous real estate agent.** Schedule informational interviews and come prepared with the specific list of questions included in this chapter. Know which answers you're looking for, and which ones should be your cue to make a hasty exit.

3. **Line up a lender.** Do not be intimidated by the bank lenders. They are in the business of making money by lending money; they love clients like you. Even if you're broke, be confident and ask the right questions.

4. **Secure a contractor.** Start with referrals if possible; if no one you know has any recommendations, get a list of previous clients from all your prospects and give each one a call. The more contractors you meet, the more readily you can spot the guy whose personality and skill set best match your project.

5. **Consider offering monetary incentives for early completion.** This is a great way to stick to your time line and keep your team fired up.

5

BUILDING A BUDGET

Flip·o·nom·ics (flip-ə-ˊnä-miks) *n.*   The (sometimes) scientific approach to managing your flipping funds.

After painstaking research and a laborious but fruitful interview process, you've assembled a formidable crew. Your Realtor's sharper than your Henckels Pro Series High Carbon Stainless Steel paring knife. Your lender? A god among men. And your contractor? You're still shaking your head at the luck of finding such an honest, articulate, skilled soul with room in his busy date book for you and your project. Bravo!

Your team thusly installed, we come to the mother of all questions, the core of your new career, the foundation for your flip.

How much money can I make at this?

The answer to that question depends on approximately 16,000 variables including, but not limited to, what you pay for your house, what comparable homes are going for, how well and how wisely you fix it up, how hog wild you go with your renovations, how long it takes you to complete the work, how aggressively you (or your Realtor) market it, what the real estate market in your area is doing, how meticulously you track your expenses . . . the list truly is endless.

Scenario A: You pay top dollar (say, $350K) for a complete teardown in a neighborhood in which the best homes are going for $400K. You planned to spend $30K on renovations and complete them in four weeks. Instead you spent $60K and the work took four *months*—and you didn't even install the half bath that you were hoping would boost your home's appeal. When no one coughs up your inflated $395K asking price after four months, you lower your price to $380K and finally sell. Congratulations! After factoring in Realtor fees, your mortgage payments, property tax, utilities, insurance, and closing costs, you only lost about $70K on that deal.

Still want to give this flipping thing a shot? If so, you might just have the stomach for this business.

Scenario B: Your hard-working, famously connected Realtor finds you a foreclosure, and you pay the fire-sale price of $400K for a nice pad in need of some updating. (Completely "done" homes in this area are going in the $525K range.) After sitting down with your contractor and discussing all the necessary work, you come up with a seven-week time line you both feel is doable. You determine your budget by creating a line-item list of the necessary expenses—and then you double it, for good measure. Based on your educated estimates, you budget $45K for renovations.

Two weeks late and barely over budget, your wisely priced house sells at the first open house—for $515K. After shelling out the fees previously mentioned (plus the obligatory capital gains tax), you walk away with $35K.

That's $17,500 a month. More than $4,400 a week, or $610 a day (even on days you weren't working—although there may not have been many of those). Not bad, wouldn't you say?

First, the bad news: There's a lot that I can teach you to help you avoid experiencing Scenario A, but as in life, there are no guarantees. You can do everything technically right and still lose your rear end. It certainly wasn't my greatest concern at the moment, but in the tragedy of 9/11, I lost $700,000. Part of that loss was my fault: I broke one of the cardinal rules of flipping ("Do not get emotionally attached") and way overspent. I bought the house in question for just under a million dollars and lavishly threw an additional 900,000 (borrowed) dollars into it. I spared no expense and created my dream home. The "house that eBay built," as I fondly called it, sported a front door that had once welcomed visitors to a farm in Minnesota and a bullet-riddled tin ceiling straight out of a saloon in North Dakota. I filled that house from the baseboards to the rafters with extraordinary antique fixtures, priceless stained glass, original this and authentic that. I knew that someone would come along and love it as much as I did and be willing to pay a premium for it.

I actually forgot somewhere along the line that I had planned to sell this house. I got so emotionally lost in the flip that I didn't notice my budget dancing right out the window. I designed rooms for my unborn children, envisioned the fabulous parties and holiday dinners my future family would enjoy there. It wasn't until the place was move-in ready that I was quickly reminded that we couldn't afford to live there.

It could have worked out okay. It was a rapidly rising market and the house was so stunning that I might have been able to price it at above what I had in it and still make a profit. Sadly, that's not what happened.

I had just put my dream house on the market at $2.5 million (a more than fair price considering the work I'd done, the quality of the materials, and the ritzy hood it was in) and got an immediate full-price offer. But my buyer's funding didn't come through and escrow didn't close, so I had to bring it back on the market. My timing couldn't have been worse. Two days later, terrorists brutally attacked the country, and the entire nation was gripped with panic. It took about 30 seconds for the real estate market to grind to a halt. The payments on my charming little eBay bungalow were over $10,000 a month, and needless to say, I couldn't afford to carry it indefinitely. In addition, I had already closed on a replacement property and was ready to close on a third house I was planning to flip. I had no choice but to slash the price and sell my dream home. At the time, I was considered lucky to get $1.8 million for it. Seven hundred thousand dollars less than I was counting on.

Ouch.

I cannot protect you against disasters. The market unexpectedly tanks? You're on your own. But I can walk you through the flipping process, give you a clear idea of the expenses you'll need to consider, and repeatedly highlight such critical components as *buying your flip at the right price, not getting emotionally attached,* and *pricing to sell.*

This chapter outlines the basic costs of buying and selling a house. Again, I could fill 10 tomes, each the size of the New

York City phone book, with examples and personal anecdotes and still not cover every possible scenario. I can't say across the board, "The kitchen cabinets will be fine with a coat of paint, but the windows need replacing." I can't tell you which loan to go with or which contractor to hire or whether you're paying too much in closing costs. Costs and fees vary from state to state and region to region. Interest rates are impossible to generalize or predict. The market changes constantly as does supply and demand. And houses are as unique as the people who buy and sell them.

That being said, whether you're talking about a 2-bedroom condo in Kentucky or a 10,000-square-foot house in South Beach, there's an unavoidable list of expenses you can expect when you flip it. On the following pages, I go through that list, but please do not think that reading this book is a substitute for doing your local homework. My book won't jump off your coffee table and scream that you're about to overpay for a particular property, and it is unlikely to tap you on the shoulder when you're creating your budget to remind you that you forgot to include homeowner's insurance. We're in this together, and I'm expecting you to do your part. *Capiche?*

The Basic Costs

When you're flipping a house, you first are going to buy it; then you will simultaneously carry (meaning make the mortgage, insurance, utility, and maintenance payments) and renovate it; and finally you're going to sell it. After that, I hope you're going to write Uncle Sam a fat check to cover the capital gains tax. (I hope you will do that because it will mean you made some decent jack.) Each action has its own

79

associated costs, which we go through here and use to create a sample budget.

Here are the basics, in easy-to-digest outline form:

- Down payment
- Inspections
- Appraisal
- Closing costs (buy)*
- Carrying costs
    —Mortgage
    —Utilities
    —Maintenance
    —Property taxes
    —Homeowner's insurance
- Renovations
- Staging
- Closing costs (sell)*
- Realtors' fees**

*Buyer and seller usually split closing costs, so you'll pay (your half) twice.

**Sellers usually pay the buying agent's and the selling agent's commission, so you score when you buy but take a hit when you sell.

Don't be overwhelmed. It just looks like a lot. All right, it *is* a lot. And yes, there's some math involved—but it's basic. Addition, subtraction, multiplication, division. There are no Pythagorean theorems, no opposite-of-b-plus-or-minus-anything, not a single formula involving the infinitesimal pi. Your third grader could do it, so go get him if you have to. Full-blown arithmophobia (and that's an actual word meaning the fear of numbers; Google it if you don't believe me) is not going to get you out of this exercise.

For illustrative purposes, I have created a fictitious scenario that we will follow throughout this chapter, so you can see the process in action. (I'll even do the math for you this time around.) To that end, I introduce you to Casa Kemp, the ersatz estate you just purchased for $200,000. "Done" homes in CK's hood are going for around $310,000. With the combined beauty of foresight and fiction, we know for a fact that you can complete all the renovations and get it back on the market in four months' time.

Let's see how much profit you're going to make here.

Your Down Payment

Questionnaires always like to ask: Rent or own? Well, if you rent, it's pretty clear. You make a payment every month to the black hole that is your landlord's wallet for the luxury of having a borrowed roof over your head. You get no tax breaks, build no equity. It's the CDB (Cost of Doing Business) in Leasing Land.

So if you don't rent, surely you must own. After all, it's right there in black and white, one-or-the other relief. The reality is, most people who "own" a home actually own only a very small part of it, at least initially. The standard down payment is 20 percent, so if that's your initial investment, that's how much you own. The bank or lender owns the rest, and not until you pay it off is the whole kit and caboodle truly yours.

I bring this up for a reason: When you're buying a house that you are planning to live in, possibly for several years or even the rest of your life, putting a huge chunk of cash down on it lowers your monthly payments or possibly even shortens

81

the duration of the loan. It is a long-term ownership strategy, and for many people, it's a good one.

When you're buying with the intent to immediately sell, you may not have any money at all to begin with. In that case, your only option is 100 percent financing. You'll pay a higher interest rate than if you had a down payment because the lender—who will in effect own 100 percent of the property—is also taking 100 percent of the risk. But if you are approved and can swing the monthly mortgage payments for the amount of time you think you'll be carrying the loan, this is a great option for first timers.

If you have some money to put down, you'll almost certainly earn a lower interest rate. At that point, if you need additional funding for your renovations, you can take out an equity line of credit (in an amount close to your down payment). Since all the interest is tax deductible, this is probably a wise move if you have access to some cash.

After looking over your finances, you decide you really can't afford to put anything down on Casa Kemp, so you finance the entire purchase price ($200,000). At 6 percent interest only, your monthly payments will be $1,000, or $4,000 for the four-month carrying period.

Inspections and Appraisals

Between the time that you write and submit an offer to buy a house and the close of escrow, you will shell out for one or more home inspections and an appraisal.

The physical inspection is a thorough once-over of the property done by a licensed contractor or home inspector. Depending on the size of the property and your area of the country, a physical inspection can run anywhere from about $200 to $700. They'll check the roof, the plumbing, the electrical work, and the foundation; look for mold, rot, cracks and leaks, and generally give you an idea of the state of the place. Your inspector may recommend additional checks by specialists. The house may need to be tested for mold, radon, or lead; the land the house is on may require a geological or soils inspection; and if there's a hot tub or pool, it's a good idea to have all of the equipment tested by an expert. If an inspection unearths something that's a deal breaker for you, all you've lost is the cost of the inspection. (Money very well spent.)

While I advise never skipping an inspection, I also suggest going for a limited scope if you know you'll be making substantial repairs. A quickie inspection will cost you less than a thorough check, so why not save a few bucks where you can? The inspector should do a thorough reinspection once you have finished your work but before it hits the market, so you can catch any red flags before your potential buyer's inspection.

On Casa Kemp, you paid $350 for your physical inspection (just one because you're only doing cosmetic repairs), and another $150 for mold/lead testing. (Both came out fine. Congrats!)

Before your lender starts shelling out any coin, the loan officer wants to be sure your property is actually worth the price you are paying for it. That's where an appraisal comes in. Expect to pay $500 to $1,000 for an appraisal, but don't necessarily expect to see a bill for this. It varies from lender to lender, but appraisals may be rolled into the cost of the loan, rather than billed as an out-of-pocket expense. Just be aware that this is something you're paying for. For our illustrative purposes, let's say you paid your $750 appraisal fee on Casa Kemp out of pocket.

Closing Costs

When it comes time to close on your property, it may seem as if everyone and his brother is waiting for a handout. They are. All these fees together make up your *closing costs*. These charges can and do vary widely, but on Casa Kemp, here's what they amount to:

Escrow fees. Who will pay escrow fees (buyer or seller) is usually decided during the negotiation on the sale. Splitting these fees, as you arranged on both the purchase and sale of Casa Kemp, is common. You'll pay half—for our example, budget $700 in your initial closing and half again ($700) when you go to sell.

Credit check. Yes, you have to pay for your lender to verify your loan worthiness (seems like a cost they might absorb, but alas, no). Set aside $75 to cover it.

Document prep fee. Again, one might assume that the mortgage and escrow companies could pay their own employees to prepare your documents, but once more you get the honors. Budget another $75 for this expense.

Recording and notary fees. For another $75, you get a nice, official raised seal on all your paperwork certifying that a living, breathing human was paid for the privilege of watching you sign all 274 pages of your purchase and loan agreements. It is not optional, so be prepared to cough it up.

Title insurance. A lender won't give you any money without guaranteeing its interest in the property. Title insurance covers you in the unlikely event that there's a blemish on your property's title history. An example: A search unearths an error on the deed transferring ownership of your lovely little flip from the previous owner to your seller. Although two generations ago the property was owned jointly by a married couple, only the husband's signature was recorded on the transfer records. Technically the wife could still make a claim to the property. She almost certainly wouldn't get it, but there could be significant legal fees involved were she to try making a claim. Obtaining title insurance on Casa Kemp (at the bargain-basement price of $400) protects you from this, and you probably won't get your loan without it.

Miscellaneous fees. A courier is employed to transport your paperwork from the title company to the escrow company. Money is wired from your lender to your seller's account. Your lender incurs an underwriting fee and naturally passes it on to you. At Casa Kemp, you're charged all these fees plus a few others, but fortunately you factored in $300 for such incidentals.

  Toolbox

COMPARING COSTS

Online calculators can be a great aid when you're trying to estimate your closing costs. You can play around with the numbers and instantly see how changing just one variable affects the overall picture (kinda like an Excel spreadsheet, but everything's already laid out for you). Check out the closing cost calculator at http://www.loanpage.com/morclose.htm to see what I mean.

Carrying Costs

Your carrying costs refer to what you pay to own and maintain the property. Consider them monthly expenses and review them often as an incentive to get your work done quickly and avoid writing another round of checks. Carrying costs break down as follows:

Your mortgage. This payment represents the largest chunk of your carrying expenses. Remember, you put nothing down on Casa Kemp so you're financing the entire loan amount. Your fabulous lender scored you a nice 6 percent interest only loan, which means you'll pay 6 percent of the purchase price every year in interest. That works out neatly to $12,000 a year, or $1,000 a month. That adds up to $4,000 for the four months you'll be renovating it.

Property tax. Since your house isn't edible (let's hope), you will be taxed on it. Figure one percent of the purchase price annually. On Casa Kemp, that's $2,000, which equals $167 a month. Since we are going to carry the property for four months, we need to factor $668 into our budget.

My 10th-grade algebra teacher had a sign on her desk that read, "If you fail to prepare, prepare to fail." If Mrs.

Snyder ever decides to flip a house, she'll probably make a mint. Case in point: Shortly after you purchase your property, you will receive a property tax bill. It may seem shockingly low, but don't whip out your dancing shoes. Your first bill will be based on what the previous owner paid for the property. Let's say she bought Casa Kemp 20 years ago for $25,000. The initial tax bill will be for a paltry $250 (1 percent of her purchase price) for the entire year. Once the new purchase info has been recorded with the county, it will waste little time sending you the bill for the difference ($1,750). Know it's coming, and it won't blindside you.

Homeowner's insurance. It's the last bastion of legalized gambling, and you can't get a loan without it. (Otherwise, since the majority if not all of the property will essentially be owned by your lender, they lose their shorts if disaster strikes.) For all intents and purposes you're betting that either a drunk driver will drive through the front door, a skunk will sneak in and spray your new carpet, or a band of rogues is at this very moment planning to break in and steal your brand-new, high-end stainless steel appliances. Your insurance company, on the other hand, is wagering that the world is indeed a friendly place and that everything is going to be hunky-dory.

Homeowner's insurance varies by region and extent of coverage. On Casa Kemp, we're paying one-eighth of one percent for top-notch coverage. That translates to a grand a year, or $83 a month. For the four months she'll be yours, that's $332 out of your pocket.

Utilities. My guess is your crew probably won't be hip on working in headlamps and toting massive water buckets to

87

work with them each day. That means you'll want the electricity and water hooked up and ready to go on Day One.

You probably don't need to hook up a phone because everyone has a cell phone anyway, right? Not necessarily. I flipped a house in an area that got pitiful cell reception and wound up having to install a "mobile office" (essentially a dumpster with utilities). You must have access to a phone on a job site, not just to order materials and stay in touch with your crew but to comply with safety regulations. If you know that mobile reception can be dicey, factor a land line into your costs.

I suggest getting the cable up and running as well. Even if you don't plan to have plasma TVs blaring MTV at the open house, it's still a worthwhile move. In fact, I just finished renovating a house where the cable lines hadn't been updated in 30 years. When I plugged in my TV, the reception was dreadful. The local cable company came out, dug new trenches, and ran new lines—all at their expense. I could advertise "brand-new, updated cable!" and it didn't cost me a dime. The crummy condition of the old lines might never have even come up during the inspections, but I felt much nicer knowing I had been thorough, and you can bet my buyer appreciated it.

Your utility bills can vary greatly, but for Casa Kemp's three bedrooms and two baths, budget at least $150 a month, or $600 for the duration of the work.

Maintenance. It's not a huge expense, but it is one that is often forgotten. Do you think the house is going to clean itself, the lawn will conveniently remain clipped and watered, and any weeds in the vicinity will decide to holiday in the south of France while you complete your work? You can do all this work yourself, but if you find your time is better spent elsewhere, it'll save you some headaches to budget for maintenance. Around $300 should cover you for four months.

So, to recap, so far we have spent:

Purchase price	$200,000
Inspections	500
Appraisal	750
Closing costs (buy):	
Escrow fees	700
Miscellaneous fees (total)	925
Other carrying costs:	
Mortgage	4,000 ($1,000 × 4 mos)
Utilities	600 ($150 × 4 mos)
Maintenance	300 ($75 × 4 mos)
Property taxes	668 ($167 × 4 mos)
Homeowner's insurance	332 ($83 × 4 mos)
Total	$208,775

Renovations

Here's an honest-to-goodness conversation I had with a client:

ME: So what's your plan here?
JOE CLIENT: Well, I bought this place for $400,000 and I'm going to sell it for $500,000.
ME: Why, that's a delightful plan. Good for you! What are you basing your selling price on?

JOE CLIENT: The fact that I want to make a hundred
  grand!
ME (TO MYSELF): Oh, Joe, Joe, Joe.

Joe is in for an unpleasant surprise. He hasn't given a moment's thought to taxes, insurance, or Realtors' commissions.
He probably doesn't know exactly what he is going to do to
his house in terms of renovations, what that work will actually cost, or what price he might get for his renovated pad in
that realm of existence we call reality.

Sellers are blind. We invariably think our charming little
two bedroom on a postage stamp is worth far more than the
sprawling five bedroom with the view on the flag lot down the
street. It's not. We also try to look at a house and see how
much work it needs and base our improvement budget on
that. In my experience, it just doesn't work that way. (Not if
you want to make any money, that is.)

Establishing Your Renovation Budget

There is no hard-and-fast rule for determining your renovation
budget, but my best advice is to back into it: First, establish a
reasonable time line and use it to total all the costs described in
this chapter. Now, using all the market research you have com-
piled over the past few weeks and months, determine what
"done" comps are going for in your neighborhood.

---

*The key to determining your renovation
budget is the answer to this question:
How much can I really get for this place?*

You want your selling price to be about 2 percent less than the closest comps to guarantee a quick sale, and thus keep those gnarly carrying costs to an absolute minimum. (Casa Kemp's comps are around $310K, so we're going to aim for a list price of $304K.) Take your selling price and subtract all the costs previously listed; what's left is a combination of your improvements and your profit.

If you aim to spend half of that amount on improvements, that leaves the other half for your profit. There's always the chance that your finished product will be worth more than you anticipate (here's where every flipper envisions an open house morning headline screaming, "Market Up 20 Percent Overnight!" followed by a frenzied bidding war with a dozen bids coming in at tens of thousands of dollars over the asking price). You can hope for such fortune, but don't bank on it. Look at your profit potential realistically, and it will become a lot clearer that maybe the existing cabinets can be rehabbed (and thereby retain their undeniable charm and character) for a fraction of the price of ripping them out and putting in custom equivalents.

So now the question becomes, how much do you want or need to make on this flip? What is it worth to you? This is where you learn to strike that delicate balance between making money and doing a good job. Your goal is to do both. You don't want to make a lot of money by cheaping out at every turn, and you don't want to make zilch (or lose money, heaven forbid) because you went hog wild and splurged on extravagant extras that no one but you will appreciate. Remember, you're selling a feeling, not a Kohler toilet. If seeing that logo is extremely important to you, buy the Kohler seat and slap it on top of the perfectly good existing john (as long as it's not stained, chipped, flamingo pink, or sporting a brass flusher that clashes hideously with all your new oil-rubbed bronze fixtures).

The details of your renovations are covered in Chapter 7, but for now, we're going to subtract the total of our estimated buying, closing, and carrying costs ($230K) on Casa Kemp from our selling price ($304K). That leaves us with about $75,000 to split between renovations and our own paycheck. If we spend $50K on renovations, we walk away with $25K (before taxes). If we reverse that scenario and spend $25K, we score (pretax) $50K. Now, I ask you: Do you *really* need to have that inlaid marble fountain out back—or would you rather put that $2,000 toward the vacation you're going to need when this project wraps?

For our example, we're going to split the difference: Of our $75K, we budget $37,500 for renovations (which would ostensibly result in an equal amount in well-deserved revenue). Because of our hard work and diligent planning—and because it's really hard not to—we only go a tad over ($40,000 on the nose).

I admit that there have been many times when I've sacrificed a few of my profit dollars because I just couldn't let well enough alone. I've even occasionally made a conscious decision to make a little less money by making my flip a whole lot nicer. If you know you won't be subject to such temptation, you've already got a leg up on me. I get so much satisfaction out of making things beautiful that it can be a curse. When that happens, I try to say, "Okay I only made $2,000 for two months' work but the house looks phenomenal and I learned a lot and I met some incredible people, made some killer contacts, and my buyer isn't going to sue me." To an extent, you determine what you're going to walk away with. Keep that in mind when you're deciding whether to rehab or replace.

For Casa Kemp, we chose a price of $304,000 because that is 2 percent less than comps selling at $310,000. Another tactic would be to price it at $299,999. This accomplishes several things: It attracts those buyers who have set $300,000 as their cap (and most buyers choose a round number for their outside limit); it gives you a psychological edge because technically your price is still in the "twos"; and if your property is worth considerably more, this strategy *may* ignite a bidding war that results in a final selling price that's even higher than your original asking price. There are no guarantees, but it's an option. For now, we're going to stick with $304,000 because the numbers are easier to run.

Staging

Staging is just fancy flipper talk for decorating your place, and you'd be amazed by what it can do for your bottom line. First timers may have to get creative here. That could mean borrowing your own or friends' furniture to fill the space (assuming you or they have marvelous taste and your cat hasn't used your couch as a scratching post). It could mean combing garage sales (hit the nicer neighborhoods for jewels) or—if you're planning to make a career out of this—investing in a few key pieces.

One of the first houses I flipped was a basic three bedroom. I only had two beds to use for staging, so I stuck a table and chairs in the third bedroom. After the first open house, I got several messages from baffled Realtors saying that they thought my listing said it was a *three bedroom*. Now, if the folks whose job it is to count closets couldn't make this quantum leap, surely my potential buyers couldn't either. So I sprang for the new bed and sold the house the very next weekend. Would it have sold anyway? Who knows? But as a rule, don't expect buyers to do their own thinking. You're leading the way, my friend. And staging is how you do it.

Staging takes the empty shell that is your house and turns it—in your buyer's mind—into a home. It makes rooms identifiable and personal. ("Remember the room with the trundle bed?" They'll muse. "We could put little Jack's crib right under the window!") Now, if you have lousy taste or crappy furniture, it's not going to help your sale. Not sure if your stuff is acceptable? Scour the 17 Pottery Barn and Restoration Hardware catalogs that choke your mailbox each week. Their rooms are warm and inviting. They draw you in. They're usually filled with lots of neutral, clean pieces and accessories. Emulate these rooms, draw inspiration from them, but don't copy them directly. You are not Rooms To Go. Familiar feels good, common does not. Rent a few key items if you don't have the right stuff, and try to pepper your rooms with interesting finds like vintage rugs, colorful lamps, or unique artwork.

We're going to use mostly our own furniture at Casa Kemp (okay, and a few borrowed pieces—thanks, Mom!). We'll drop a strategic $2,000 on standout accessories that will blend in beautifully with our own stuff at home when we're done.

Real Estate Agent Fees

You got a break on your buy because the seller paid both his own and your Realtor's fees. But when you sell your finished masterpiece (unless you negotiated otherwise), the bill falls into your lap. The two Realtors involved will split the standard 6 percent commission. If one Realtor worked for both sides, she gets the entire 6 percent. (This is the one time I make an exception to the "no discounted commissions" rule. If your Realtor is acting for both the buyer and seller, it is fair to ask her to take 5 percent since the orchestrating of schedules has been eliminated.) On CK, which you sold for your asking price of $304,000, commissions to the two Realtors total $18,240.

Pest Inspection

It is usually the seller's responsibility to provide buyers with a pest inspection. This includes (again, unless otherwise negotiated) completing any repairs caused by bugs, fungus, or dry rot wherever there is *visible* evidence of infestation. These repairs are known as "Section 1" work, and most lenders require their completion to close escrow. The inspector's report may or may not include recommendations for "Section 2" work, which is indicated when conditions are deemed likely to lead to problems (excess moisture conditions, faulty grade, etc.).

Here's a small incentive to get your work done fast: Most pest reports are good for 90 days, so if you turn over the property within that time, you may get to skip this expense. If it's been longer than that, call the company that inspected the property when you bought it; since they're familiar with its recent condition, you may get a better deal on a reinspection.

If a pest company determines that work needs to be done, they may give you an estimate for the repair work—but that doesn't mean you are obligated to use them. You can do the work yourself or get your handy brother to do it for a fraction of the cost. Either way, you must bring the pest company back after the work is finished so you have a certificate of completion to show to your buyer.

Pest inspection prices vary depending on the size of the house (and of course, the hood it's in). We paid $300 to have CK reinspected and another $200 to take care of our Section 1 responsibilities.

Capital Gains Tax

This is where your painstaking tracking of receipts comes into play. If you hold the property for less than two years, the IRS classifies the sale as a short-term capital gain. Therefore, the profit you make on your sale will be taxed as ordinary income (which means at 28 percent or higher, depending on your tax bracket). After the two-year mark, you're allowed certain tax-free gains (up to $250,000 for a single person and $500,000 for a couple). For this reason, some flippers make a habit of buying and holding for two years. As long as you factor this tax into your budget, whether you hold or sell will depend on your long-term goals and strategies. *Consult your tax advisor.*

Every penny you spend buying, carrying, renovating, and selling your pad gets subtracted from the taxable total, so leave no stone unturned. With Casa Kemp, our expenses (or "cost basis") totaled $270,215. (Remember, even though we financed 100 percent of the original purchase price, we have to pay off that loan when we sell, so that's $200,000 to the bottom line.) Subtract that number from our sale price of $304K, and the amount we're going to be taxed on is $33,785. Assuming we're in the 28 percent tax bracket, we'll be greasing Uncle Sam's palm with $9,460 and change.

Here's how the whole deal breaks down at Casa Kemp:

Purchase price	$200,000
Inspections	500
Appraisal	750
Closing costs (buy):	
Escrow fees	700
Miscellaneous fees (total)	925
Other carrying costs (4 mos):	8,000
Mortgage	4,000 ($1,000 × 4)
Utilities	600 ($150 × 4)
Maintenance	300 ($75 × 4)
Property taxes	668 ($167 × 4)
Homeowner's insurance	332 ($83 × 4)
Renovations	40,000
Staging	2,000
Realtors' fees (6% of sales price)	18,240
Pest inspection/repairs	500
Closing costs (sell)	700
	$270,215 cost basis

Sell for	$304,000
Costs	270,215
Gross profit	33,785
(This is the amount you'll be taxed on.)	
Capital gains	9,460
(28 percent of GP)	
Net profit	$24,325

Congratulations! You made it through your first flip and took home a nice little paycheck. We're talking more than $6,000 a month for your four months of work, after tax. (That translates into an annual salary of more than $100,000—not too shabby.)

Now, remember. Carrying costs on Casa Kemp total $1,475 a month. That's almost $50 a day. Had you decided to take two weeks off during the renovation, it would have cost you $700. Had you put it on the market at an unrealistically high price and let it sit for three months, that move would have run you $4,425 in time (not to mention losing potential buyers who went on to find something else). This illustrates the need to (A) be efficient and (B) price your house to sell.

Chapter Summary

1. **Establish your projected sale price.** You do this by researching sales of homes that are comparable to yours in size, specifications, location, and amenities. Homes that are slightly under priced sell faster than those priced at or above market value.

2. **Work backward from your projected sale price to create your renovation budget.** Subtract the purchase price, capital gains tax, carrying costs for the estimated construction period, and real estate agent commissions; what's left is a combination of profit and improvement costs. Ask yourself: How much must you make to consider this flip worthwhile? The rest represents your renovation budget. Can you improve the property significantly with that amount—enough at

least to get your projected sale price? This is the make-or-break question.

3. **Determine your down payment.** The more you put down, the lower your carrying costs but the less you have for improvements.

4. **Compute your closing costs.** As a seller, you will more than likely have to pay your share of the closing costs including escrow fees, your credit check, document prep, recording and notary fees, title insurance, and other miscellaneous fees. You may need to finance more than the purchase price of your home if you don't have the necessary cash.

5. **Calculate your carrying costs.** This figure represents your monthly outlay to maintain the property and includes your mortgage payment, utilities, maintenance, property tax, and homeowner's insurance.

6

CREATING A TIME LINE

Flip·out (´flip-out) *n.*   A momentary judgment lapse that leads you to believe you can rebuild an entire house in three weeks.

I have to fight the urge to start every chapter, section, and paragraph with the sentence, "The biggest mistake flippers make is . . ." Because all flippers, myself included, make copious mistakes. Alas, one of the granddaddies of oversights is inefficiency. I've said it before, but it can't be overemphasized: Time is money. It is often the last thing people consider and the first thing that can ruin your flip.

Too many times, I have stood on a property with a buyer who had closed the day before, and it is quieter than a morgue at midnight. I show up expecting to see hustle and bustle, tools, and Porta-Potties, and instead I am surrounded by frightening stillness. Nothing at all is going on.

Although it involves some preplanning, your work should start on Day One if at all possible.

PREPLANNING

When I write my initial offer, I always add a condition to my contracts along these lines: "Buyer to have access to house five times before close of escrow with 24 hours' notice to seller." This lets you take stock of the place; measure for windows, flooring, and cabinets; and generally get all of your construction ducks in a row. If the seller isn't amenable to trespassing, factor at least a week onto the front end of your time line for strategizing. Your architect, contractor, and crew should all be present on Day One for planning purposes.

Without knowing exactly what you plan to do to your property, I can't tell you how long it will take to rehab it. Here's what I can tell you: Establish a reasonable time line by figuring out what you need to replace and what you can overhaul; then talk to your contractor and your suppliers, and obtain any necessary construction permits. Then expect that time line to change. Double it, then add a month or two for good measure, and *maybe* that is when you'll finish. If it takes you a week to rip it out, plan for two to three weeks to rebuild it. Disheartening, yes. But if you plan for the worst and hope for the best, you might just be pleasantly surprised.

Many times, I see people talking up time lines that don't seem to be based on any firm or even remotely realistic plans. "I think I can do this in three months," they'll say. Or, "My contractor friend Arthur has four weeks off and we're going to work a trade."

Well that's all well and good—until you decide at the last minute to double the size of the kitchen and order custom cabinets that come in the day Arthur's off to Aruba. What then, my friend? You have a problem. You know the saying: If ifs and buts were candy and nuts, we'd all have a merry Christmas (or the happy holiday of your choice).

I recommend working backward. (My lawyer wants me to clarify here: I do not mean that literally. If you step heel first into the cement trough that was once your property's pool, I am not liable. Clear?) Work backward, *time wise:* Envision your open house. How does the place look on that day? How did it look a week ago when you took the pictures for the open house ads in the paper? Is it fully staged? Is there running water? Have the windows been spit shined? Are Porta-Potties still lined up on the driveway? Is leftover sheetrock resting against the garage door? If you schedule your open house for Sunday, do you know when dumpster pickup days are? If it's every other Monday and you wrapped the project on Friday, you may have just destroyed your curb appeal.

Create a Time Line

Always create a time line and put every single nitty-gritty detail you can think of into it. (And that includes trash pickup, unless you fancy frequent runs to the dump.) Out of the first ten houses I bought and sold, *eight flipping times*—pun intended—I somehow overlooked having the utilities up and running and in my name on Day One. Take it from me, there is nothing more infuriating than having to deal with a mistake for which you can blame no one but yourself.

No matter how diligent, painstaking, and downright perfect you are, there will be errors and oversights in your planning—you cannot avoid them. Windows will break, paint will chip, and plumbing will back up. What starts as a simple fixture swap will unearth dangerously dated wiring that demands to be updated—pronto. You'll rip out a wall and find dry rot, termites, mold, or all three. Or maybe the inside will be perfectly healthy, but you'll realize it wasn't the wall you intended to rip out in the first place. You hear about it in medicine all the time—the guy with gangrene in his left foot wakes up from surgery to find his right foot has been amputated. Equivalent mistakes happen in construction: Perfectly good cabinets get smashed to smithereens, mint-condition floors don't get protected because someone tells someone else they're being replaced anyway. A contractor I was working with once ripped out a vanity that I had specifically instructed him to leave intact. Fortunately, our relationship was such that he instinctively suggested the $800 for a replacement would come out of his pocket. (I agreed wholeheartedly that the $1,800 for the one I wanted should.) Such mistakes don't just cost tons of money, they also flood the job site with tension and (at the risk of sounding new-agey) negative energy.

The answer? Be on top of your job. Fix what needs to be fixed. Do the invisible but necessary repairs first. As eager as you are to start hanging that lovely leopard wallpaper, you need to hold off until all the boring mechanical stuff is updated and brought up to code. Yes, land mines are lurking everywhere. But with some luck and the info in this chapter, I hope you can sidestep at least a few of them.

You know those organizational and managerial skills you boasted about on your resume? Now is the time to put them to the test. As soon as I start a flip, I start a to-do list. I leave lots of blank spaces for notes and for inserting items I invariably forget. For a basic cosmetic flip, the rough initial list might look something like this:

- Utilities (have turned on)
- Waste disposal (order dumpsters)
- Demo (industry shortcut term for demolish or demolition)
- Appliances (order)
- Lighting
- Patching
- Counters (kitchen/bathroom(s))
- Tile (backsplash)
- Floors (wood, linoleum, carpet, tile)
- Bathroom fixtures
- Hardware (cabinet pulls, doorknobs, hinges)
- Paint
- Landscape
- Open house prep

Start making your phone calls to determine how long each item will take from beginning to end. Include demo, ordering, measuring, installing, and invariably reordering. Remember Murphy's Law? If something can go wrong, it will.

Your delivery guy *will* run a red light and get broadsided and all your custom windows will be reduced to rubble. Bank on it.

For an average or midsize three-bedroom/two-bath cosmetic flip with the mechanics and innards intact, figure on a minimum of three weeks to get the necessary work done. In making that estimate, I am assuming two things: (1) You are ready to go on Day One and have your crew lined up with tools poised; and (2) you have three full-time laborers, each of whom is well-rounded enough to do more than one job. Think about it: If Eddie the Electrician knows squat about plumbing and diddly about drywall, you've got to line up two other specialists and wait for their schedules to open up every time a detail arises that doesn't fall into Eddie's realm of expertise. The more experience you or your laborers have, the more time and money you'll save.

The last three houses I've flipped involved more than just paint and plaster. They were all built in the 1970s and hadn't been updated since. We're talking worn shag carpets, choppy floor plans, no overhead lighting, dark, paneled walls, and ugly aluminum windows. Enough to make any eager flipper jump for joy.

I always refer to my flips by the name of the street they're on. The time line and rough costs for Natoma, the last of the disco-era flips previously mentioned, broke down like this:

Purchase price: $1,239,000

Time	Activity	Cost ($)
Week 1	Take "Before" photographs	
	Activate utilities	
	Have dumpster delivered	
	Demo kitchen and baths	

Time	Activity	Cost ($)
	Begin lighting (recessed)	
	Open kitchen wall	
	Labor	3,500
Week 2	Order tile for kitchen and bath	4,300
	Order door hardware	1,200
	Buy microwave shelf cabinet	59
	Investigate permit for exterior demo	
	Demo potting shed	
	Arrange cable wiring	
	Order bar stools	96
	Order kitchen table	800
	Order appliances	5,000
	Order back door	262
	Measure and order window treatments	5,500
	Labor	3,500
Week 3	Finish recessed lighting	1,300
	Upgrade all electrical wiring for steam unit	800
	Order couch	1,700
	Install kitchen faucet	250
	Labor	3,500
Week 4	Demo concrete in front and rear yards	250
	Lay out deck	1,300
	Begin crown molding	450
	Begin plumbing baths	2,000
	Install bathtub	450
	Labor	3,500
Week 5	Finish crown molding	
	Build bath and kitchen countertops	1,400
	Begin landscape irrigation	2,000

(continued)

Time	Activity	Cost ($)
	Prep for tile in baths	
	Order master bedroom headboard	400
	Labor	3,500
Week 6	Remove old iron fence around front yard	
	Remove rear porch railing	
	Interior and exterior paint prep	5,000
	Order new iron fencing	1,200
	Upgrade electrical panel	250
	Buy plants for front and rear yards	800
	Labor	3,500
Week 7	Paint interior	2,500
	Pull up carpet and sand hardwood floors	3,500
	Order shower glass	1,800
	Plant hedges	
	Labor	3,500
Week 8	Begin building rear deck	
	Stain hardwood floors	
	Install Roman shades in kitchen	
	Buy breakfast table and chairs	1,000
	Paint exterior	2,500
	Labor	3,500
Week 9	Finish deck	
	Install tile in bathrooms	
	Choose grout color	
	Finish hedging	
	Grade yard surface	
	Apply second coat of stain to hardwood floors	
	Retrieve remaining furniture from storage	
	Stain and seal countertops	

Time	Activity	Cost ($)
	Hang drapes	
	Arrange couches and beds	
	Install doors and hardware	
	Clean	400
	Labor	3,500
Week 10	Complete heating evaluation	
	Touch up paint	
	Purchase remaining furniture and accessories	2,000
	Install kitchen floor	600
	Purchase plasma televisions	5,000
	Touch up landscaping	
	Install shower glass	
	Install front fencing and gate	
	Clean	250
	Remove dumpster	2,000
	Take "After" photographs	
	Labor	3,500
	Carry costs, maintenance, and utilities	7,000

Remember, Natoma was built in the 1970s, before "lifestyle" was a buzzword in home design. The entire front yard and backyard were seas of concrete, which not only is aesthetically off-putting but also doesn't have families jumping for joy. I got a few bids on the concrete demo and realized it would be cheaper to have one of my guys break it up than to bring in a specialist. This is where running the numbers pays off. It took three days of jack-hammering, a day of hauling, and two full dumpster runs (at a cost of $1,000 to unload the concrete) to get the job done. But once the new sod and plants were in place, the payoff was immediately evident.

The inside was equally lacking in charm. The kitchen was a dreary, isolated box completely cut off from the rest of the living area. Ripping out half a wall and creating a pop-thru to the kitchen area was an easy, relatively inexpensive way to bring this house into the twenty-first century. I topped the half wall, which separated the kitchen from the family room, with a piece of mahogany and voilà! Instant breakfast counter with seating for four.

I was tempted to completely demo the kitchen cabinets, but in reality they were perfectly functional and the floor plan worked. By simply staining the existing oak trim on the doors to match the new mahogany breakfast bar, the entire kitchen got a face-lift and I didn't have to replace the countertops or wait six to eight weeks for new cabinets. I installed a combination microwave/hood above the existing range to open up more space on the counters, found a linoleum remnant for the kitchen floor that worked with the scheme beautifully and added a new faucet and soap dispenser.

Then there was the back door. Opening up the kitchen to the front of the house improved the traffic flow and aesthetics, but there was still an issue of light. I decided to spring for a new single-pane clear glass door to replace the solid wood one that led to the backyard. Not only was the entire house instantly flooded with light, but now I was able to advertise "new exterior doors" because I had replaced one and the front door was in good enough shape to appear new in my marketing materials. That one door revolutionized the whole space, for the bargain-basement price of $189 and just a few hours' work. Always look for opportunities where you can bring in light (and cash; see Figure 6.1).

Every once in a while—certainly not as often as disaster strikes—but it happens nonetheless, your flip house will reveal a

(Before)

A dated but functional kitchen needs a cosmetic boost.

(After)

Figure 6.1 The kitchen goes from blah to brilliant with new lighting, appliances, paint, and a new back door. An added bonus: Window coverings transform the feel of the space for very little money.

hidden treasure. At Natoma, the nasty, worn-down, wall-to-wall avocado carpet was obscuring glorious hardwood floors that hadn't seen so much as a single footstep. A word of caution if you are lucky enough to discover such a hidden jewel: As enticing as it may be to reveal and revel in the floor's beauty immediately, remember that the old carpet serves as a fabulous, protective work surface. Drag tools across it and drip paint from one end to the other if you're so inclined. Then pull it up after all the dirty work is done, and you'll still have pristine floors.

I also saved a big chunk of time and money on Natoma by not replacing the underwhelming windows. Instead, I splurged on custom window treatments and crown molding, two things I could then advertise to set myself apart (and together still way cheaper and less time-consuming than buying and installing 16 new windows). I tucked inexpensive curtain rods behind the molding, creating a cozy look; and I saved money on fancy decorative rods in the process. Not only did these elements conceal and shift attention from the existing windows, but they gave the whole house a high-end feeling and left buyers with the impression that I'd gone the extra mile.

Natoma was equipped with two lackluster bathrooms. The smaller, uglier one was attached to one of the bedrooms, making it by default the master suite (even though there was nothing masterful about it when I started). I knew I somehow had to make that little water closet feel special, so I took advantage of the undersized shower by splurging on swanky tile (the small space worked in my favor) and adding a steam unit. The latter set me back $1,400, but automatically catapulted the shower into the "spa" category, thereby adding several thousand dollars of value (see Figure 6.2).

In the other bathroom, I replaced the shower with a tub/shower combo, which added a lot of appeal for not a lot

(Before)

(After)

Outdated finishes call for an update.

Figure 6.2 New paint, hardware, fixtures, a wood countertop, and glass tile backsplash deliver major impact and create a high-end feel.

of time (a half day) or money ($162, to be exact). By surrounding the ho-hum tub with eye-catching tile, the bathroom took on a designer vibe. I kept the existing sink and toilet, repainted the vanity, installed new light fixtures and floor tile, hung a handsome mirror, and slapped on a new toilet seat—a must in every flip if you are going to recycle the old bowls. Check another room off the list.

After I painted the walls, tore up the carpet, and sanded and stained the floors, I wisely budgeted a day for cleanup. People frequently forget about this when planning their budget and time line. When you get to this point in your flip, you may be tempted to invite a few Realtor acquaintances or friends of friends or maybe even the whole damned market to check out your digs. *Do not give in.* It is essential to have every last finishing touch—from the fluffed-up throw pillows to the almighty apple pie baking in the oven—before you unveil it to anyone. Once you load in all the furniture, plan at least one more day of cleaning to let the dust settle yet again.

A final, critical element in your schedule is the timing of your sale. As you are nearing the end of your renovations, sit down with your Realtor to discuss the marketing plan. How can you drive the heaviest possible traffic through your front door? Is it better to hold an open house before other Realtors see it on caravan? This will vary from area to area, so count on your Realtor and other trusted professionals to guide you. Again, it is paramount that the house be completed before the first potential buyers and their agents see it. You only have one chance to make a first impression, and if there are leftover construction materials lying around or blue tape covering the hardware or an overflowing dumpster in the driveway, you haven't given your property the awesome debut that translates into a quick sale (see Figures 6.3–6.4).

(Before)

A dysfunctional, closed-in, and unattractive backyard.

(After)

Figure 6.3 Adding a deck, sod, paint, and taking away the ugly awning adds major value.

(Before)

Old carpet protected the original hardwood floors in this 1940s ranch house.

(After)

Figure 6.4 Newly sanded floors, crown molding, designer lighting, and a pop out in the wall open up the living room/dining area and revolutionize the entire feel of the space.

Purchase price	$1,239,000
Total renovations cost	100,317
Sale price (appraised)	1,650,000
(kept as short-term rental property)	
Potential profit after fees	175,500

So, to stick to your meticulously planned time line:

- Start work on Day One.
- Manage your expectations.
- Be present on your job site daily.
- Stay organized.
- Maintain a clean job site.
- Work backward from your open house day.
- Take time for some rest and renewal to perform at your best.

Chapter Summary

1. **Start as soon as possible.** Don't start racking up credit card bills the day your offer is accepted, but the minute your contingencies have been lifted, you can and should begin planning. Work backward from your projected open house date and make sure you schedule time for often-overlooked jobs like cleanup, photos, and open house preparation.

2. **Weigh your options.** Do not begin demo until you have realistically determined what you can rehab and what you should replace. Every time you remove something—cabinets, walls, trim, windows—it costs time and money to put something else in its place.

3. **Focus on the mechanical before the aesthetic.** Updating the electric wiring and securing the foundation may not be glamorous, but these tasks must get done—and the sooner, the better. Likewise, as eager as you are to install your new bamboo floors, the minute they're in place you have to take steps to protect them while the rest of the work is being completed. Stick to a time line that makes sense and you'll be much better off in the long run.

4. **Create a to-do list.** Include room for arranging utilities and dumpsters, demo, ordering and installing materials, painting, landscaping, and cleanup.

5. **Be realistic.** Things will go wrong, materials will get lost and broken, unexpected complications will arise. Allow time for such mishaps, and you'll handle them in a much calmer, more effective manner.

6. **Time your sale.** Do not allow a single soul (other than the penniless friends you know aren't going to buy) through your front door until every last detail is in place. You only get one chance to make a first impression.

7

IMPROVING THE PROPERTY

Flip·serv·ice (flip-ˊsər-vəs) *n*.   The conscientious manner in which serious flippers attend to a property's every detail.

One of the reasons I enjoy investing in real estate so much is that it is tangible. I can touch it, feel it, smell it, live in it. How many stocks can you say that about? If you have even the tiniest atom of design ambition in your blood, the hardest part of your flip will be memorizing and living by this simple mantra: Less is more. As in, the less of the existing structure you demolish or remove, the less money you spend replacing it and the more you take home.

It all comes down to balancing perfectionism with professionalism. By this point, I hope I can safely assume you know

I'm not suggesting you hide structural flaws, use inept labor-ers, or comb dumpsters for free fixtures. But if your turn-of-the-century farmhouse has charming, well-worn butcher block countertops that blend in perfectly with the rest of the period details, don't rip them out or plop a cheap Formica slab on top of them, even if you think it looks better or "newer." If the white appliances are in good physical and me-chanical shape and will disappear into the cabinets once you paint them Linen (that's the fancy paint word for the color white), dropping $15,000 on stainless steel appliances may be a waste of precious time and money.

Remember, potential buyers will only spend a half hour or an hour inside your flip before they decide whether to make an offer. You want them to leave with the impression that everything is "new" and "done," even if the only reason it is sparkling is because you scrubbed it silly or slapped on a fresh coat of paint.

Don't Overpersonalize

Another major mistake flippers frequently make is overper-sonalizing a space, which usually translates into overspend-ing. Do I need to remind you of the eBay money pit again? It is critical that your finished product have a personality and sense of design, but it also needs to be neutral enough to ap-peal to the masses. It seems oxymoronic: You're trying to appeal to a buyer's emotions, yet I'm asking you to leave your own emotions out of it. Striking that balance is admit-tedly tough.

I once had a footwear-obsessed client tell me she was planning to create an entire room in her flip house for shoe storage. Well, that's all well and good, Imelda Marcos, but save such extravagance for the dream house you can afford to build for yourself after you've flipped a few houses successfully with the mass market in mind.

Joe Buyer and Lucy Looky-Lou may not know how to execute good taste, but they likely know it when they see it—they get those Pottery Barn catalogs, too—so it's your job to create it without busting your budget. How, you ask? A good start may be to find a new development in your area and check out the model homes. Pay attention to the color schemes they're using (can you say *neutral*?). Notice the details that catch your eye and proclaim "well-done." Maybe you love the pasta-pot spigot over the stove or the custom built-ins in the closet. Do the dual shower heads leave you weak with lust? Make a list of these emotional triggers and figure out which ones will make the most impact in your flip.

If your house is oozing with charm, maybe buyers will overlook the fact that there's no spa tub in the master bath and no oversized apron sink in the kitchen. But if your house is a boring box at the core, you are probably going to have to spring for a few interesting accoutrements. Remember that some things (dishwasher, forced heat, sprinkler system, relatively updated appliances) are a must if you don't want your buyers to feel as if they're getting last decade's model and if you expect them to pay the premium you are hoping for.

Home decorating catalogs are another way to stay on top of current paint colors and fixture finishes. When in doubt, go for pale earth-toned walls (taupe, butter, beige) with Swiss Coffee (a.k.a. ivory) trim. Can't decide between brushed nickel and weathered bronze hardware in the bath? Consult an associate at a store like Restoration Hardware or scour the pages of the online or print Rejuvenation catalog (www.rejuvenation.com), where items are conveniently grouped by era. Above all else, make sure all your hardware accents—and that includes the previously mentioned toilet flusher thingy as well as doorknobs and hinges—are the same. (You can paint the hinges the same color as the door, but knobs should be replaced if they don't match the rest of the metal accents.)

If you must experiment with interior design on this flip and you haven't been told you have a gift for it, keep it simple with one accent wall that is easy to paint over, or toss some fun and funky throw pillows onto a window seat. You can't afford to gamble on there being one other person on earth who fantasizes about having lime-green marble counters or one-of-a-kind, hand-blown glass sinks and who will not only walk through your open house but have the desire and cash to buy it on the spot.

High Impact, Low Cost

This is another area where confusion often arises: Clients frequently tell me they read an article that says you get 100 percent of your investment back if you improve a bathroom. That deceiving statistic implies that you're making a killing, but in fact, it simply means you're breaking even. Let's say you have $10,000 to spend on renovations. If you put that money in a nice, safe savings or money market account, you could probably earn maybe 3 percent a year. That's $300 profit—not a windfall, but better than breaking even. At every turn, ask yourself how your money can make you the most money. I have received the greatest return from investing in the following three improvements:

1. Enhancing curb appeal.
2. Updating kitchens and baths.
3. Increasing the flow of a floor plan by taking down walls between kitchens, living rooms, and dining rooms. The great room is a great way to sell your buyer on today's lifestyle.

When you start getting caught up in the frenzy that flipping can create, you must find a way to rationalize sticking to your budget and not going all-out. Remember my brand-new condo? The "finished" pad I couldn't resist personalizing? As impossible as it is to believe, for every buyer who wants a turnkey property, there's another who is just itching to put his personal stamp on his new home. I once had a buyer pay me full price for my flip, then proceed to absolutely gut—down to the bare studs—the beautiful kitchen I had built. Fifteen thousand dollars of brand-new tile, counters, and cabinets were sledge hammered and replaced without a second thought. Never mind that those solid walnut cabinets had been custom built for the space, or that I'd painstakingly chosen and mounted all 38 pieces of hand-forged hardware. You never know what ideas your potential buyers may have in their crazy heads. Keep that in mind when you decide, "My flip stops here."

You cannot ask yourself this question often enough:

How can I enhance what is already there?

With each flip, think back: What were your first thoughts when you set foot on the property? Ostensibly, you chose the house because of its overwhelming potential. Focus on what it has before determining what it needs. Did you bushwhack your way through overgrown weeds to find what could be a charming lit-tle front porch? Did you walk inside and immediately realize the choppy floor plan could be fixed by simply removing one useless wall and creating a massive, open kitchen/family room? Maybe you understood that finishing off part, or all, of the attic and adding a closet or half bath would catapult you into a new price point. You will make the most money by capitalizing on the promising details that called out to you in the first place. If the kitchen layout works, but the cabinets and finishes need updating, you will save money by replacing them but keeping appliances near their original locations to avoid replumbing and moving electrical lines and outlets.

 Toolbox

KITCHEN DESIGN

Can't decide whether to demo the existing kitchen? Look first at the layout. Ideally, the refrigerator, sink, and stove should be laid out in a triangle so you can get from any one to another without having to take too many steps. Having them all lined up in a nice, neat row means any countertops will be at the farthest ends, making any culinary task akin to a stint on the treadmill. Also in this perfect world, the triangular formation will include counter space on either side of the stove, next to the fridge on the side that the door opens, and on either side of the sink.

Where to Stop!

You will also need to consider how your planned changes affect the rest of the space. Perhaps you want to replace the vanity with a pedestal sink, but you didn't necessarily plan to replace the flooring. Can you match that 1940s art deco tile exactly when you go to fill in the gaping hole around your new sink base? Maybe you're thinking about swapping out some windows. Find out first if the existing ones are standard sizes, as custom-built windows can cost two or three times more than prefab ones. Assuming you have carefully constructed your budget, you can easily determine how such splurges will impact your profit margin. Some nice drapes may suddenly sound like an excellent alternative.

Many flippers have elaborate fantasies of adding extra space to their properties. Perhaps you picture a widow's walk, guest wing, or sunken sunroom off the master suite. My advice:

Think twice before building up and out.

Anytime you change the "footprint" of the house, your expenses escalate. You're no longer renovating, you're rebuilding. That means permits and electricity panel upgrades and foundations and surveys and lots of money. Unless you're the lone one bedroom on an avenue of mansions, you'll invariably turn a healthier profit if you work with what you've got.

So how do you know what to rehab and what to replace? I always strive for a combination of form and function. Anything that stays had better be in perfect working order. Once that has been determined, I ask myself if there's any way I can make it look better. Solid wood cabinets may just need a fresh coat of paint and some new pulls. A boring, all-white bathroom might look positively spa-ish with new bronze sink hardware, complementary light fixtures, and a sumptuous shower curtain. No one's saying it wouldn't look even better with a skylight and slate floors, but if that's not in the budget, good enough has to be good enough. Tossing a pretty, oversized throw rug on the floor instead of a boring old bath mat is a great distraction tactic. First-time flippers are constantly amazed at how little it can take to transform a room.

Your house's inherent style and the era in which it was built will play major roles in the transformations. Nothing drives me crazier than when clueless renovators carelessly equip their Spanish hacienda with modern chrome fixtures or drape heavy velvet swags across their ranch house's no-nonsense windows. A talented designer can pull off that eclectic mix and make it look intentional, but a flip house is not an outlet for your first swing at cutting-edge design. As much as you might pine for a jetted Jacuzzi tub, a vintage claw-foot model is a much better match for a craftsman-style home (and might end up saving you a few bucks to boot). If you are not willing to do the research necessary to determine what improvements will be in keeping with a home's architectural style and integrity, do not flip that house (see Figures 7.1–7.3).

Recognize Your Flip House

It is important to define your house so that buyers can label it and make it memorable among the list of 10 to 20 houses

(Before)

Scalloped trim and an embellished garage door date this 1950s ranch house.

(After)

Figure 7.1 New glass in the windows, an updated garage door, fresh paint, and clean landscaping provide great curb appeal.

(Before)

This living room with carpet and no architectural interest is in need of an updated look.

(After)

Figure 7.2 Hardwood floors, crown molding, and staging create an inviting space for gatherings in the living room.

(Before)

Dated cabinets and the brick fireplace cry for a total upgrade and restructuring of the space to open it up.

(After)

Figure 7.3 Removing a row of cabinets and installing high-end appliances were essential in this high-end neighborhood.

they may be considering to buy. "Oh, honey, but I loved that Victorian house with the updated kitchen" means *money* in your pocket.

Perhaps the beat-up gem you have your eye on may lend itself well to one of these recognizable, classic designs:

Cape Cod
1600s–1950s. The Cape Cod style originated in New England in the late seventeenth century. Today, the term refers to one-and-a-half story homes popular in the United States during the 1930s, 1940s, and 1950s.

Antebellum Architecture
1830–1862. Antebellum is not a *style* so much as an *era*. These grand plantation homes reflect the wealth and power of plantation owners in the American South before the Civil War.

Victorian Gothic
1840–1880. These buildings feature arches, pointed windows, and other details borrowed from medieval Gothic cathedrals.

Victorian Italianate
1840–1885. These houses represent Old World ideals transplanted to the United States.

Shingle
1874–1910. Home designers rejected fussy Queen Anne ornamentation in homes that evoked rustic coastal living.

Colonial Revival
1880–1955. These symmetrical houses combine elements of Federal and Georgian architecture.

Mission and California Mission
1890–1920. Stucco walls, arches, and other details inspired by the Spanish mission churches of colonial America.

Tudor, Medieval Revival, and English Country
1890–1940. Decorative half-timbering and other details inspired by medieval building techniques.

American Foursquare
1895–1930. This practical, economical style became one of the most popular in the United States.

Prairie School
1900–1920. This low, linear style was pioneered by Frank Lloyd Wright.

Craftsman Bungalow
1905–1930. A product of the Arts and Crafts movement, this American style was popularized through mail-order catalogs.

Spanish Revival
1915–1940. The opening of the Panama canal inspired Spanish Colonial Revival and Mediterranean styles.

French-Inspired
1915–1945. French ideas reflected in grand estates and quaint cottages.

Art Moderne
1930–1945. Smooth, white walls and a sleek streamlined appearance, these cube-shaped homes express the spirit of the machine age.

Ranch

1935–Present. The rambling, no-nonsense Ranch styles became dominant in the United States during the 1950s and 1960s. If you live in the suburbs, there's a good chance your home is a Western Ranch, American Ranch, or California Rambler.

Raised Ranch (Split-Level)

1935–Present. A traditional Ranch house is only one story, but a split-level, Raised Ranch house has room to grow. A finished basement with large windows creates extra living space below, while a raised roof leaves room for bedrooms above.

More information about these house styles can be found at the following web site: http://architecture.about.com /library/bl-styles_index.htm.

 Toolbox

GO GREEN

Scores of recycled or energy-efficient materials are available today, and they don't always cost more than their synthetic equivalents. Using plasters made of mud, Lo voc paints, floors made of cork or bamboo, insulation crafted from cotton or straw or countertops of poured concrete will enable you to market to an ecologically concerned clientele—and surpass your competition by doing nothing other than making a few smart substitutions. That being said, keep your bottom line in mind at all times.

Dig for Gold

Your goal when shopping for your home's improvements should be the same as it was when you were shopping for the home itself: To pay the lowest possible price for the highest quality materials. Heard there's a new architectural salvage depot opening next week and it's within a day's drive? Be the first one there for the grand opening with your 50 percent off coupon clutched tightly in your hand. Stop by building supply shops and salvage yards, and develop relationships with the owners. Once you do, you might say to the latter, for example, "I'm on a budget and am looking for a stained glass front door from the 1920s. Can you keep your eye out for me?" The more people you have working with you, the more likely you will take home an exceptional find for a song.

Although it's not as easy as it once was to get amazing pieces at online auctions, I still land remarkable deals on eBay. Yes, I know lots of folks revolted against eBay's fee hikes and switched over to the auction arm of sites like Overstock.com, but I still prefer eBay for the sheer volume of merchandise. Back in the days when most sellers weren't virtual "e-tailers" but folks looking to unload some junk they found in the garage, you could score amazing deals by intentionally misspelling your search item and crossing your fingers. The online community in general has gotten significantly more sophisticated since the inception of auction sites, but there are still bargains to be had.

Please remember that I do not make a living hunting down or hawking random tchotchkes online. Therefore, this book does not include a comprehensive reference section detailing every facet of Internet auctions. I am not a power seller. I'm just a gal who's raised her virtual paddle often enough to have learned a trick or two. If you really want to make a career of online shopping, there are hundreds of books on the market that can help you hone your auctioning skills. I'd suggest searching on Amazon.com for books about eBay, and reading the reviews to find the title that best matches your interest and experience. In the interim, here are seven secrets I wish I had known the first time I hit that "bid" button:

 Toolbox

BECOME A CHAMPION eBAYER

1. Decide what something is worth to you before you start bidding—then stick to that price. Even if it looks like you lost by a penny, you'll never know what the other bidder's top bid might have been. Tell yourself it was thousands of dollars more and move on.
2. Never bid with a round number. Many bidders will set, for example, $20 as their maximum bid. By entering $20.02 you may win by a nose.
3. Don't bid on anything until the last minute. Bidding early does nothing but raise the item's price and tell other potential bidders you're interested.

4. If you can't be at your computer when the auction ends, consider joining e-snipe (www.esnipe.com). For a nominal fee, their computers will bid for you at the last minute, so you don't have to sit—and stress—in front of your computer. You pay just 25 cents for winning auctions under $25, 1 percent of the price between $25 and $1,000, and a flat fee of $10 for anything above that. You pay nothing if you don't win the item.

5. Research similar items. Bidders get emotional; don't get wrapped up in the competition of winning a bid—you still have to pay the price you "won."

6. Consider shopping for parts instead of completely assembled items: Buy a light fixture's back plate from one auction, the chain from another, and a mica fixture that's missing the first two parts from yet a third. Put them together with some pliers and you have a premium fixture you can advertise as authentic.

7. Don't be lazy. If an item matches your search description but doesn't have a thumbnail photo (or displays a fuzzy, unprofessional one), take the time to check it out. You'll often find hidden treasures this way simply because other buyers won't take this extra step.

Now your home is complete. You have sacrificed time with family, friends, and your "paying job" to get it done. And if you made the right choices, your hard work will pay off handsomely: You deserve to be compensated for your efforts. The kitchen is fashionable and functional, the bathrooms are modern and marvelous, the walls and floors are pristine. So how are you going to draw potential buyers through the front door? Two words: Curb appeal.

Curb Appeal

The truth of the matter is that it doesn't matter what you've done to the interior of a house if you can't get buyers out of their cars. When it comes to a home's exterior, your goal is to create a feeling of expansiveness and privacy. That means lawns and fences. I'm a huge fan of sod; after paint and elbow grease, it offers the biggest bang for your buck in terms of instant transformation. If ripping up a sea of concrete isn't in your budget, at the very least, you must break it up with clusters of potted plants. Would a nice picket fence give your home's façade the charm it is missing? This is just another inexpensive fix to consider.

If space allows, there should also be an area somewhere on the property for some hardscape—a deck or some flagstone where a table and chairs can serve as an outdoor entertaining area. This is especially important if you live in an area with moderate year-round temperatures. Adding that patio practically adds another room to the house, without the budget-crushing expense of walls and a ceiling. It is also the secret to selling a lifestyle. When potential buyers come through and can see themselves entertaining on the back porch with that very table and chairs, they are much more likely to write an offer.

If you are forced to dig up the yard to put in a sprinkler system on a timer (something today's buyer expects in a finished home), consider adding a gas line for a built-in barbecue. It won't cost you much once the trenches have already been dug, and you don't necessarily have to install the actual barbecue. Just roughing in the gas line will be enough for you to use it as a marketing tool and increase the value of the house.

Outdoor lighting is a tricky issue. On the one hand, strategically lit landscaping can add valuable drama to your home's look—but it may be money needlessly spent unless you decide to hold your open house at night (or you live in Alaska). If you do go the extra mile, make sure your marketing materials prominently feature photos of your property's after-hours allure.

Tips for Improving Your Home's Exterior

- Ensure the address numbers for the house are clear and visible from the street.
- The location and path to the front door should be obvious from the moment your buyers pull up. The walkway should be free of tree roots, debris, gaps between stepping-stones, and grass waiting to be pierced by stilettos.
- Are the windows clean and has the paint that spilled over from your fresh trim been scraped off?
- What greets your buyer at the front door? An inviting bench? A contemporary light fixture? A front porch covered in Astroturf? (The latter is not encouraged.)
- Lay new sod or reseed old grass to make it appear green and devoid of bare spots. Pick one or two types of flowers and stick to a monochromatic theme for the landscaping. A smattering of impatiens lining the front

walkway does not say "high end" or designer, and you may lose your buyers before they even set foot in the entryway.

- If the front door is dated, find the money in your budget to replace it. Nothing says "cheaped out" like a front door from the 1950s with new millennium glass and hardware. If it doesn't seal tight, look right, and function perfectly, you may turn off potential buyers at the precise moment you need to grab their attention.

- Are there telephone wires draped across your front lawn? Consider investing in having them buried or plant a mature tree near by to distract from the eyesore that is the phone company in your yard. Fruit trees are always a good option because they are colorful, smell great, and in a pinch provide lemons for homemade pie. I like to include useful plants in my landscaping such as rosemary, tomato, and lettuces.

- Do the exterior colors complement each other and the houses on either side of yours? Be sure and pick a neutral tone that will serve as a backdrop against your fresh landscaping.

- Create privacy by installing fences on the perimeter of the property and softening them by planting hedges or vines in front of them early on in your project so they are grown in by the time you have your open house.

- Update the mailbox with paint or replace if it is dented. Nothing says pride of ownership like a shiny new mailbox.

Figures 7.4 show one property before and after new landscaping.

(Before)

An overgrown fence offered no curb appeal and hid the home's architectural charm.

(After)

Figure 7.4 New paint, landscaping, and the removal of the old fence reveals a charming home and highlights the mountain views.

Tips for Profitable Improvements

- Less is more—don't go demo crazy thereby forcing yourself to replace everything you just demolished. Whenever possible, enhance what is already in place to save time and money.
- New paint can do wonders to freshen up any house. Pick neutral, warm, and inviting colors and try your hand at varying the shades a bit from room to room. Paint large spaces (kitchens, dining rooms, great rooms, and hallways) the same color and paint the ceilings lighter than the wall color.
- Don't overpersonalize but appeal to potential buyers' emotions (her: new kitchen; him: workbench in the garage). You never know what a buyer's hot button might be, so if possible, include low-cost extras such as two sinks in the master bath and storage under the stairs.
- Find a way to add a designer's touch to your flip even if this is not your forte: Go to open houses, visit model homes, flip through catalogs for design ideas and inspiration.
- Make sure the hardware trim on cabinets and interior doors is consistent. Few things look more unfinished than mismatched doorknobs and bin pulls.
- Know when to stop. If you've tapped out your budget, have the discipline to stop spending and start getting the house ready for sale.
- Determining the layout of a house is paramount before you can start getting excited about dreamy finishes. Budget to change the flow and floor plan if it is dated

or does not function for today's modern buyer before you splurge on a new tub for the master bath.

- Know and study the style or era inherent to the house. It could help guide you toward finishes that will suit your completed project.
- Shop eBay or garage sales for finds that are reasonably priced but original. This will set your property apart from other houses on the market at your price point.
- When the work is complete, clean the house and then clean it again a few days later after all the construction dust settles. You should also consider having the water pipes examined and cleaned out to avoid any unexpected backups caused by construction materials obstructing the new plumbing.

Chapter Summary

1. **Keep your eye on the prize.** Remember, your goal is to make a profit. You do that by spending the least amount of money in the least amount of time while turning out a professional-looking product. Enhance what is there. People will pay handsomely for a "done" house; going overboard rarely results in a massive windfall for a flipper.
2. **Check out model homes in your area.** Not only will you see what your buyer will use for comparison with your house, but you might find a few key design and decorating ideas.
3. **Try to work with the existing space.** Adding rooms can be a costly endeavor. Before you break new

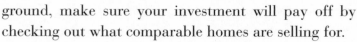

ground, make sure your investment will pay off by checking out what comparable homes are selling for.

4. **Consider your home's inherent style.** Don't fill a country cottage with modern trimmings, or a ranch house with Victorian antiques. Some styles complement one another and some simply clash. Consult an interior designer if you're not sure which way to go.

5. **Add small, thoughtful touches.** Ripping out the drywall in the bathroom anyway? Install an electrical outlet in the back of a drawer so her blow dryer is always plugged in, or put a niche next to the john to hold the toilet brush and extra toilet paper.

6. **Be Switzerland.** If you keep your material choices neutral, you'll appeal to the broadest possible segment of the market. Neutral doesn't have to mean boring. It just means saving the cobalt-blue backsplash or chartreuse wainscoting for your own home. Add drama with accessories and accents (pillows, towels, flowers, etc.) that the buyer can easily see through.

7. **Don't forget about curb appeal.** Your house has to look as good on the outside as it does on the inside if you hope to get potential buyers through the front door. A clean yard, some colorful foliage, and an inviting entryway are minimum requirements.

8

STAGING YOUR FLIP

Flip·a·de·do·da (flip-ə-dē-dü-´dä) *n.*   The catchy little tune you'll be singing when you first lay eyes on your finished, decorated flip.

When Holly and Harry Homeowner put their house on the market, ostensibly it's filled with all their worldly possessions. This can be an asset or a liability, depending on the Homeowners' personal sense of style, their definition of cleanliness, and their propensity to be packrats. But generally speaking, a furnished, *finished* home sells more quickly and easily than an empty box, even if the latter has twice the potential.

The way to make your recently renovated, vacant house feel like a home is by staging it. Again, this is another place where you have to take a good, hard look at your talents, taste, and strengths. If guests to your home constantly compliment your decor or ask for your opinions when purchasing items for their own homes, chances are you've got the gift. If, however, your pad is furnished with stackable plastic crates, lawn furniture, or a smattering of Papasan chairs, and your wall art consists of unframed concert posters (and you see nothing wrong with any of this), *you are going to need help with staging.*

Staging creates the illusion that your home is occupied by an impossibly neat, enormously stylish, wildly design-oriented family or individual. Staging gives a house personality but doesn't anchor it in an overly distinct style. Personality isn't expensive or permanent. If buyers don't like your taste, they should be able to see past it, but if they do like your taste, it should make them want to buy the house even more.

The goal of staging your flip is to get your full asking price or better yet, even more. You're tugging at all of your buyer's senses with the feel of velvet throw cushions, the visual pop of a gorgeous print or flowing drapes, *a place to sit and write an offer.* Literally. I once watched my buyers sit down in the dining room I had only at the last minute decided to furnish and do just that. A first-day sale was well worth the price of a table and some chairs.

Think about who is likely to buy your property. A one-bedroom fourth-floor walk-up downtown will attract a vastly different crowd than a five-bedroom split-level ranch home in a neighborhood rife with parks and preschools. An army of stuffed animals on display is only appropriate in one of these two scenarios, and if I have to tell you which one, you may want to reconsider your new hobby choice.

The moving in of furniture and accessories may not happen until all the renovations are complete, but you should be planning how you will stage your flip from Day One. If you know in advance how you're going to allocate each room and have figured out how the bedrooms will be set up, it will help you lay out everything else, particularly electrical outlets and switches. If you're planning to set up a conversation pit in the center of the living room, put an outlet in the floor. It's a small touch, but it can make all the difference in the world if potential buyers aren't tripping over a spaghetti-tangle of cords when they inspect the house. Figure 8.1 shows how tasteful furnishings and accessories can add to the appeal of a room.

Deciding What to Put Where

Making layout decisions in advance also allows you to determine what can be camouflaged and what needs to be completely repaired and restored. No one is intimating that if you plan to put a sofa on the south wall you can skip the chair rail back there. Nor is anyone suggesting that you install plantation shutters and then promptly glue them shut in the hope that no one will notice the cracked panes of glass behind them or the unlovely view of the *Sanford and Son* shack next door. But let's just say you were on the fence about whether to completely refinish the decent but not exactly to-die-for hardwood floors in the living room when you scored a gorgeous, enormous throw rug at a garage sale that will fit the room perfectly. Do you want to create the overall impression of hardwood floors or of gleaming, brand-new, hand-finished bamboo floors that may seem out of place in the context of the rest of the space? As long as you are not trying to hide gaping cracks or other major flaws, your $10 rug may have just saved you $1,000.

(Before)

Cold walls and no furniture make this dining area stark.

(After)

Figure 8.1   The addition of new fixtures, warm colors on the walls and windows, designer furniture, and some plants give this space a welcoming, finished feel.

Window coverings are a big part of staging, as fabric is a simple way to add texture, warmth, and a splash of color for very little money. If your house lends itself to the cottagey look, installing crown molding six inches from the wall can allow you to tuck inexpensive curtain rods behind it, saving you tons of money in decorative window hardware while creating an elegant look.

But wait a minute! Your flip has big, beautiful, fabulous windows! They're a selling feature and you'll be damned if you're going to cover them up! Well, my friend, you *are* going to cover them if the view they afford consists of nothing but your neighbor's ramshackle RV moored in the driveway or the crumbling cemetery across the street. If, instead, there's a nice patch of landscaping out there, can you install a simple window treatment to complement the color of the camellias lining the frame? Or would the house actually feel bigger and more open with bare windows? Consider the entire picture before locking into tab tops in every room just because that's what you have in your own home. Figure 8.2 shows a room before and after being staged.

Your Local Bookstore Will Be Full of Ideas

Your local bookstore is your best friend when you're planning your design strategy. You could spend weeks flipping through the piles of *Architectural Digest* gathering dust in your study, or you could simply hone in on a book dedicated to, for example, French Country kitchens or Art Deco bathrooms and save yourself a lot of hassle. Make notes on the color schemes and accessories that catch your eye, and start a file. You'll refer back to these a thousand times before

(Before)

An empty living room strains potential buyers' imaginations.

(After)

Figure 8.2   Adding furniture and accessories allows buyers to picture themselves living in the space—an emotional pull to purchase the home!

you've finished your flip. Bonus: Books that relate to your home's architectural style or the work you've done make fabulous staging pieces strewn atop a coffee table or lined up on bookshelves, so consider them a worthwhile investment in more ways than one.

Don't have the aforementioned coffee table or bookshelves yet? You need a plan. There are several ways to acquire or accumulate furnishings for your flip. You can use stuff from your own home, borrow from friends, scour flea markets and garage sales, splurge on pricey custom pieces, engage in some combination of all the preceding—or you can get really creative.

Where Did You Get That Furniture?

I once filled an entire flip with furniture that I borrowed from a high-end store in exchange for promoting the business with a stack of flyers at the open house. I paid for pickup and delivery, which was pennies relative to what I got in return. This was a shop I had frequented many times before, purchasing items for various clients, so I had a great relationship going in. Nevertheless, if you see or hear of a new furniture store opening in town, you may find that they will jump at the chance for a little exposure. It certainly doesn't hurt to ask.

On another flip, I couldn't decide if a couch and rug I had my eye on were just right for the house, so the store let me take them out on approval. The timing wasn't intentional and I'm a little embarrassed to admit this, but it just so happened that I was still in possession of the pair when my open house rolled around, and the house also coincidentally happened to sell at that very first open house. I returned both pieces promptly and didn't have to pay a dime. I guess if you do this as often as I do, every once in a great while you're bound to get lucky.

Another option is to advertise your needs on a local community web site, such as Craigslist.com. People may be willing to lend you their for-sale furnishings in exchange for the exposure your open house presents. You may have to pick up and return these items if they don't sell, but it's a low-cost, creative way to stage your home.

If your budget has enough wiggle room to allow you to purchase furnishings, you'll need to think about what you'll do with these items after you sell the house. How much will it cost you to secure a storage unit, or will you already be in escrow on your next flip? Accumulating a bunch of stuff you have no place to store can be an expensive problem. Do the math: Suppose you spent $2,000 on furnishings. If a storage space will cost you $230 a month and you know you're not going to finish your next flip for six months, it's going to cost you $1,380 to store that stuff—less than buying it all again. If your next flip is going to take 12 months and is smaller than your current one, you might as well try to sell the furniture with the place rather than drop $2,760 to store it for a year.

Perhaps the house was furnished when you purchased it. Often, eager sellers will throw in some or all the furnishings during the negotiation phase. You will usually have to request this. It's unlikely that the seller will be throwing extras at you unless he is *extremely* motivated or the stuff is particularly ugly. Can you toss a stylish slipcover over that ratty couch or paint the frame on the picture they left hanging in the master bedroom and make it blend with your new decor? Maybe you, and you alone, can make the funky-colored kitchen tile work by hanging a light fixture with a matching shade, or adding some coordinating accessories like hand towels and a throw rug. The more you work with what you have, the more money you'll make.

Just as you can't forget about the outside of your property when you're doing the renovations, neither should you ignore it when staging. Any kind of outdoor hardscape adds value to your property, but can your buyer visualize how to use the space? You can help by installing or cleaning up the deck, enclosing the yard, and putting in a charming little bistro set or portable fire pit. These inexpensive touches will be well worth the investment when potential buyers stroll around the property and can picture the alfresco brunches or cocktail hours they'll be enjoying there.

In case you hadn't noticed by now, shopping will be an integral part of the staging process. For some people, this is the ultimate gift-with-purchase; for others, it will be sheer torture. Everyone must know someone who lives to wake up before the roosters on Saturday morning to get the prime garage sale pickings. *Use your connections!* Consider offering a "finder's fee" for the friend who lands the perfect patio set or fireplace screen. That finder's fee could be a bagel and cappuccino, a six-pack, or a night of babysitting. Find your friends' currency and you're golden. Figure 8.3 shows how furniture and accessories can give a room personality without overwhelming it.

Accessorize, Accessorize, Accessorize

If you're serious about making this flipping business a part of your life:

(Before)

The traditional mantle and dark paint don't suit the style of this Mediterranean house.

(After)

Figure 8.3 New window coverings, a lighter wall color, and the addition of a sandstone mantle transform this space into a family room with a decorator's special touch.

---

*Start amassing accessories you can
take with you from flip to flip.*

Bedding, towels, plants, statues, rugs, coffee table books, occasional furniture, bath accessories, and the like don't take up much storage space and can be recycled indefinitely. If you've never bought or sold a house before, note that window treatments are typically sold with the property unless specifically noted otherwise.

Once again, less is more when staging. A few key pieces make a room identifiable and memorable. Too much clutter, on the other hand, feels crowded and confusing and can make even a large space seem cramped. The same goes for Olympic-sized furniture. As keen as you might be on your own California king bed, a queen will be big enough to announce "master suite" without filling the room with wall-to-wall mattress. Likewise, a twin bed and a small end table define a guest room without making it feel cluttered.

Remember, you want to project a feeling of comfort and coziness. Your buyer needs to envision living in your home. If your flip is in the top elementary school district, anticipate your potential buyer's likely lifestyle and stick a sandbox in the yard. Certain that your high-rise studio will attract only young professionals? Line the glass-front kitchen cabinets with martini glasses. Put an empty box on the market and you're simply selling air.

Staging should include some lifestyle accents and details. A tray with the day's newspaper on the coffee table, a coat rack in the foyer or a hatbox in the entryway closet are simple, homey details that provide a subtle indicator of what might take place in that area.

Your goals and budget will help you decide if you want to spring for big-ticket items and either sell them with the house or find a place to store them between flips or try to rent, borrow, or trade your way to a fully staged flip. If you buy large furniture items, be careful to avoid style-specific pieces that you can only reuse in future flips that mimic your current home's design. An overstuffed floral sofa might look divine in your country cottage, but will it be at home in the modern marvel you wind up flipping next? A basic, traditional model with clean lines in a neutral, solid color will have timeless appeal in a variety of architectural styles.

I like to bake chocolate chip cookies the morning of my open houses—the smell is intoxicating and gives buyers something to take away with them. That being said, beware of filling your house with overpowering scents, lest your guests think you're trying to mask the aroma of mold or the dead skunk in the basement. Your home should smell clean, pleasant, and fresh. Anything more can backfire.

Water features are another potential pitfall. If your flip is right next to the freeway and you stick a fountain in the backyard to distract from the traffic noise, you're not fooling anyone. Put in the fountain because it's a beautiful focal point, but price your highway-adjacent flip accordingly.

To Have or Have Not—The Appliance Question

People ask me all the time if they need to include appliances in the sale. Here's what I tell them: Appliances make a home look and feel complete. Some, such as a dishwasher, are non-negotiable. If a buyer feels stressed about filling that big, gaping hole in the kitchen, it can kill a sale. If money is that tight, you can negotiate the price of a refrigerator in your contract, but it should be present and accounted for on open house day. Same goes for a stove and dishwasher. A washer and dryer are always nice to include, but not as necessary—although hookups should be installed and tested regardless.

Another item that commonly inspires confusion is the much-maligned ceiling fan. I'm not going to lie to you: I am not a fan, pun intended. In my opinion, if you're not going to live in a house, you should choose fashion before function. There's just not an overwhelming selection of attractive ceiling fans out there, and even the best-looking of the bunch can't hold a candle to a jaw-dropping light fixture or chandelier. The one exception is on an outdoor porch, where a fan helps create a wonderful Tommy Bahama ambience. Nothing says package-store cheap like a brass fan with fake wood blades. If your flip happens to be in, say, Africa or Orlando, put in air-conditioning and call it a day. Otherwise let your buyer deal with ventilation issues as they arise. If they are less offended by fans than I am, they can always replace the vintage chandelier with a ceiling fan and sell the light fixture on eBay for a profit.

First Impressions Matter

As your open house date approaches, think about how you can make the most memorable first impression. To me, nothing says homey like a handful of live plants. I say that with one major caveat: Make sure you put the right dishes or containers underneath them to protect your new or newly refinished floors. I once placed two lovely, enormous potted plants on either side of my flip's entry hall. When I went to move my stuff out, there were two enormous spots of water damage beneath the pots and I wound up having to refinish the floors. Not the greatest way to celebrate a sale, I have to tell you.

If you know nothing about chlorophyll-exchange, hire a plant maintenance company to deliver and tend to the greenery. You may even find one who will trade the work for some strategically placed advertising at your open house. The same scenario could apply to a new caterer or florist in town. Use your brain to come up with creative ways of saving money while assembling a fantastic team of vendors. The promise of future business if you plan to make flipping a career can help sweeten the deal in the eyes of service providers.

Details that show you've thought of your buyer's comfort and happiness will go a long way. A couple of towels and a bowl of potpourri in the linen closet, a coat tree in the front hall, and a place to toss your keys when you come in create the feeling of a comfortable, lived-in space. In fact, any time I can squeeze it into the budget, I like to build a niche in the entryway. I stage it with a pair of sunglasses and some mail to show buyers how lifestyle-friendly their future home is. Similarly, if I'm doing any electrical work, I create a charging station in an easily accessed closet. For the open house, I plug in a cell phone and a few camera batteries. Today's buyers cherish convenience. Even (or especially) if they don't have it where they currently live, they'll appreciate it when they see it.

Once your flip is finished in your eyes, it's time to invite your friends over for a test-drive. Tell them you are offering snacks and drinks in exchange for honest, practical feedback—and then take it. Provide disposable guest towels so your fluffy hand towels stay that way, and have a plunger and a can of carpet cleaning spray on hand, just in case.

 Toolbox

STAGING ESSENTIALS

1. Make sure all your appliances are in working order.
2. Window treatments make your space seem finished.
3. Create scenarios and vignettes in the most used rooms.
4. A doormat at the front door says "Welcome Home" to prospective buyers and keeps your new floors footprint-free.
5. Don't forget the curb appeal. Make sure the lawn is lush, scrape away any sloppy paint on the windows, and see that the house and grounds are clear of all construction debris.
6. Add towels and a shower curtain to the bathrooms.
7. Decorate with candles, firewood in the fireplace, and a journal and pen next to the bed. Romance your perspective buyers—it works!
8. Bake cookies and play soft music on open house day.
9. Put art on the walls in the biggest spaces.

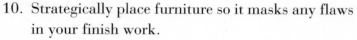
10. Strategically place furniture so it masks any flaws in your finish work.

11. Ensure the furniture you select is the right scale, preferably on the smaller side so the house appears more spacious.

 Chapter Summary

1. **Finish your flip with furnishings.** You don't have to go overboard, but well-placed pieces of furniture and assorted accessories help buyers see a home's potential.

2. **Budget already blown?** Rent, borrow, or bring things from your own home or solicit items in exchange for advertising. If you buy a few key pieces, offer to sell them with the home, or else determine how and where you will store or use them after the sale.

3. **Keep scale in mind. In smaller homes, large furnishings can make the space feel cramped.** Less is almost always more. Twin beds in kids' rooms and a queen bed in the master suite identify the spaces without overcrowding them.

4. **Start collecting.** If you plan to flip again, it may be worthwhile to invest in a collection of trimmings such as bedding, towels, rugs, and accessories that can easily be stored and recycled as necessary.

5. **Don't forget the outside.** Treat a backyard, deck, or patio as yet another room and decorate or stage it accordingly. A pair of Adirondack chairs or an all-

weather dining table can create a welcoming outdoor retreat and increase your home's usable space.

6. **Schedule a dry run.** Invite friends over and encourage them to critique your project. Ask for their honest feedback, and act on any suggestions that are within your remaining budget and time frame.

9

FLIP-FLOPS

flip·id·ity (flip-´id-i-tē) *n.*　A state of angst or regret over a poor purchasing or planning decision.

O
n TV shows, the outtakes that feature the actors cracking up, forgetting their lines, or face-planting are known as *bloopers.* Magazines and newspapers print what they term a *make-good* when an ad runs with an error or misprint that is the publisher's fault. When one or more critical aspects of a real estate rejuvenation go horribly wrong, I call it a *flip-flop.*

Flip-flops are unavoidable. They also aren't entirely un-lucky if you can evaluate what went wrong and are wise and emotionally mature enough to learn from your mistakes and avoid repeating them. It stinks mightily when you work hard; make an endless string of sacrifices; and wind up broke, brokenhearted, or both. But trust me, nothing sends a take-home message faster than a crippling financial or ego blow.

I like to think of my flip-flops as battle scars, hard-won lessons from the school of experience. When I lose money on a property, that's tuition I didn't spend going to Flipper School. When I'm on the job site until three in the morning four days in a row, those are the all-nighters I never pulled studying for my Flipping Finals. When I have to restrip, resand, and repaint the cabinets because I put latex paint on top of an oil-based primer and it turned out to be the wrong shade of beige, that's the makeup Flipping Quiz I was lucky enough to have as an option.

My flip-flops didn't all end in complete disaster, but each had its shining moment of misery. To be sure, it is sheer dig-me-a-hole agony when any part of a flip goes wrong. When the refrigerator I bought specifically because it was advertised as "counter-depth" stuck out four inches past the custom cabinets that had already been paid for and installed, thereby completely destroying the flow in my brand-new, painstakingly laid-out kitchen—and it was the day before my zealously hyped open house—I did not sit down Buddha-like and ponder the irony of bad luck or its place in the universe. When my husband decided to take a bath a half hour before another open house—the first time we tested the plumbing, mind you—and water came streaming out of the kitchen's ceiling light fixtures, I did not calmly open my demo diary and pen a witty entry under the "things that went wrong" tab. It can take hours to years, depending on the level of devastation, before I fully glean the nugget of wisdom I have gained when something goes awry.

At one time in your life, you probably have bitten into that irresistible, fresh-from-the-fire slice of pizza and singed the roof of your mouth to the point where eating was painful for three torturous days. After that experience, you can add to your wisdom database that it is not a good idea to bite into anything swimming in bubbling cheese. Not that you won't ever jump the gun again, but in theory you know better and hope to learn from the experience. In much the same way, my mistakes have made me an expert. That's not to say I never repeat them, but each encore reinforces those synapses that build the foundation of knowledge and experience.

In Chapter 5, I described the $700,000 loss I took with the "house that eBay built." Following are the details of other flips that flopped in one way or another. I hope that through secondhand osmosis, you can avoid a repeat performance.

A Flood

I just alluded to my husband's impromptu, ill-timed soak. Let me paint the rest of the picture for you. It was one of the first houses I flipped, and I had splurged on a massive spa tub in the master bath. The bath was part of a sweeping second-story addition I was enormously proud of, something you'll understand the first time you impulsively decide to add livable height to a squat but sprawling 1950s ranch house. Note to self: If you're going to dig deep footings, you'd better have deep pockets.

The magnificent master bath happened to be situated on the second floor directly above the kitchen, a fact that would have been neither here nor there had the following scenario not unfolded. There I was, passing the last half hour prior to my first broker caravan obsessively arranging and rearranging vases of already-perfect daisies when Robert announced his bathing plans. *"Now?"* I thought. But my impulsive husband really wanted to test-drive that tub, and he promised it would be dry and spot-free and that the towels would be fluffy and perfect when we opened the doors, so I agreed.

Big mistake.

Flash forward to 10 minutes until curtain time, when he pulled the tub's plug to let the water drain. Out it came, all right—straight through every single one of the kitchen's brand-new recessed can lights. You can imagine what an impression I made at my open house as visitors sidestepped the brigade of buckets scattered about the kitchen floor. King-size crimson sheets tied to my mailbox would not have been a more obvious red flag. Needless to say, I was not besieged with multiple offers that day.

The lesson: Take a shower, run the dishwasher, use the heater, turn on the sprinklers, fire up the oven, check the fans, build a fire, schedule an 11th-hour follow-up physical inspection. Your house invariably will have a few bugs, and you want to get them out *before* you show it to prospective buyers.

Mental Meltdown

I'll admit there's something I didn't really consider when I first began this journey: Even if every aspect of your flip goes off without a hitch (which happens about as frequently as a lunar eclipse), you also must contend with untold outside forces as well. You or a loved one may get sick at a critical point in the flip. Your partner could be offered an irresistible job in a faraway city or state. The market in your area may suddenly tank. Countless events can make you want to jump ship and will test your mettle in ways you cannot yet imagine.

I had scored the deal of the century by buying directly from the seller, for way under market value, a great little fixer-upper on Santa Barbara's lovely Laguna Street. I had gotten such a great deal that had I done nothing but relist it, I would have made money. That is the ultimate flip—get in, get out and make a profit before you even close escrow. But I had big plans for Laguna. I had envisioned authentic craftsman fixtures on the front porch, the woodwork in the dining room, the fire screen in front of the flames on open house day. I'd already spent about $50,000 and was up to my eyeballs in the renovations when my step dad learned he needed a liver transplant. Around the same time, I found out I was pregnant. I was nauseous, stressed out, and thoroughly exhausted. It was all too much to handle at once. A real estate agent friend, sensing my distress, offered to take Laguna off my hands. I knew I was forfeiting a massive profit, but mentally and physically, I wasn't capable of continuing. Although I felt that I had no choice at the time, I cannot drive by that house without thinking of the cash I could have made if I had just hung on a little longer.

The lesson: There will be times when you will run out of money, steam, or both. Before you bail out, make sure you have explored every option. Maybe you can stick it out long enough to break even and hang onto your life's savings. If that's not possible, at least be aware of the choice you are making. Give yourself the room to say, "I understand this isn't the ideal option, but it's the best one available to me at the time and I'm okay with it." This may save you from the shoulda/woulda/coulda breed of self-abuse that is neither healthy nor helpful.

The Ex-Con

I despise prejudice and work hard to teach my children to appreciate and respect diversity. But the day my contractor announced his new framer Al was part of an exciting new work-release program, I admit I was the teeniest bit hesitant. My apprehension must have been apparent, because I was repeatedly assured that Al was totally reformed, the hardest worker in the bunch, intent on unveiling his new and improved self to the world. I relented. What choice did I have? Where was I going to find a skilled, available framer? Plus, true to his publicity campaign, Al couldn't have been a nicer guy. And for a while, he actually did a pretty decent job.

The first time I showed up on the job and found Al asleep in the rafters, you might think I would have demanded he be fired on the spot. I did not. Maybe he has a drinking problem, I speculated. Who could blame the guy, what with the whole prison thing and all? I would just keep ignoring the dragon-in-chains tattoo on his forearm, and all would be well.

A week later, the entire crew (minus one) showed up to find that all their tools had been stolen. The drills, Sawzall, everything, gone. Not surprisingly, Al didn't show up that day or any day thereafter. To no one's great surprise, the tools eventually showed up at a local pawn shop. The shop's owner knew Al well, and as you probably discerned, confirmed it was indeed our now unreformed framer who had hocked the goods.

The lesson: Trust your instincts. Save the whales, adopt an aging, homeless Seeing Eye dog, pick up hitchhikers, do whatever it takes to satisfy your philanthropic urges. But on the job, be respectful but tough. Someone who is taking advantage of you or only giving 75 percent, does not belong on your team. Business is business, and you're the only one watching out for you. Oh yeah, and if you ever run across Al, tell him I'm still peeved. His little stunt messed with my meticulously orchestrated time line, which didn't include getting ripped off by him.

Living in Squalor

Greenworth was supposed to be a quick flip, and moving into it in all its gruesome glory was never part of the plan. But because change is the only constant in life and in flipping, we found ourselves in a pickle.

I was enormously pregnant and thrilled about it. My husband and I also had orchestrated what would have been the most outstanding of all flipping triumvirates. We were days away from closing the sale of a sweet little house we had just flipped successfully and were living in—we were ready to move into flip number two that wasn't quite complete. All the contingencies had been lifted and it was just about time to hand over the keys on our first sold flip, but, alas, its replacement was not ready. You see, even veterans make colossal planning mistakes. In fact, the house we were planning to move into was more than a month behind schedule and completely unlivable. It had unfinished floors, no heat or running water, and was no place for an expecting family and all their worldly possessions.

Fortunately, we had just closed on another house on Greenworth Lane. We briefly contemplated putting all our stuff in storage and renting a place for a few months. But to die-hard flippers, renting is financial murder, a mortal sin. Refusing to throw our money away rather than using it to build equity somewhere, we decided to suck it up and move into Greenworth while we finished flip number two. After all, Greenworth had a decent floor plan, the roof didn't leak, and it was empty and welcomed us with open arms.

Greenworth featured living conditions you wouldn't wish on your worst enemy. The entire house smelled like a urine-soaked New York City subway platform on the hottest day of the year. Floor-to-ceiling mildew in the kitchen and bathroom gave both rooms a deceptive gray-blue tint. Salivating conditions for a flipper, but not for an occupant. The scene was disgusting to anyone with working faculties, but pure, unadulterated hell to a pregnant woman.

I stayed in a hotel for two weeks, dropping more than a thousand dollars I would have much preferred to put into the house we were trying to complete. But it was a matter of preserving my health and sanity. Eventually I moved into my mom's house, a two-hour commute each way, even though I knew that a flip house must be geographically desirable and accessible.

We blew through the renovations and were making phenomenal time and progress. We could get all over-the-counter permits because we weren't changing any exterior walls, so after a few weeks, all we were waiting for were the new kitchen cabinets. Once they arrived, we could take the final measurements for the countertop slabs. Because of my great relationship with the countertop guy, he cranked out stone slabs in 10 days—a feat that usually takes three times longer. I desperately wanted to get the house on the market at the peak of the selling season—but obviously that wasn't in the cards. On his way to deliver the slabs, the counter guy hit a massive speed bump and every one of my lovely, custom-cut countertops cracked smack down the center. *Ten more days* never felt like such an eternity.

The lesson: Flipping can and will take over your life. I wound up making a mint on Greenworth (I bought it for $900K, put about $170K into it and sold it the day it hit the market for $1,395,000). Some of the items we were storing in the garage of that house did get stolen, and tragically I lost the baby I was carrying. The doctors insisted that the stress of the flip had nothing to do with the failure of the fetus to survive to term. Nevertheless, it was a heartbreaking time—and a wake-up call. You have to be committed and focused if you're going to flip successfully, but always remember what's really important to you. Money is nice; your family and your health are priceless.

Historical Shocker

When I bought my little 1919 English Cottage, its undeniable charm was what won me over. I knew that with a little imagination and a lot of elbow grease, the coved ceilings, stunning tile work and beautiful built-ins at Santa Rosa could be restored to their original glory and bring in top dollar. Little did I know that the very details that made the house so appealing would also nearly kill my flip.

It turned out that famed artist Douglas Parshall had once made my delightful little bungalow his home. Who knew? Since someone of such artistic prominence had once conducted the most personal of business beneath my new roof, apparently I was going to have to re-create his every stroke before they would let me demolish a single door jamb.

169

The illustrious history of the house on Santa Rosa made it subject to an extensive historical review that added six unexpected months to my time line. We had to go back and research not only occupancy information but period details and the life and history of the original architect as well. Then every single change had to be reviewed by a special historical review board.

Now, this was my 10th flip and I was admittedly a little cocky. It was maddening having these "higher powers" telling me where I absolutely had to put shutters and narrowing down my paint choices to an unappetizing handful. It took months of effort and energy, but I finally convinced the board that shutters on my period abode would be an abomination and that Swiss Coffee trim was indeed in keeping with the era's architectural integrity. Imagine my indignation. How dare they imply that I would consider an addition that wouldn't be in keeping with the style of the house? And where on earth was this omniscient review board when my new neighbor was slapping that monstrous, boxy second story—complete with flimsy aluminum windows and mismatched stucco finish—on top of his once-darling cottage?

Historical histrionics were only the beginning. Santa Rosa hadn't been touched since it was built in 1919. I knew from my purchasing inspections that I would have to deal with the hollow, cinderblock wall construction. My contractor estimated the work at $10,000, for which I was able to get a credit in escrow when I bought it. This part of the project was discussed at length, and it never occurred to me that the work simply would not get done. Appallingly, it didn't. And perhaps even more astonishingly, I had absolutely no idea.

This little nugget of bad news was discovered after I had a hungry buyer on the hook. His inspections unearthed the unfinished work and I was floored. I tried to offer the same $10,000 credit I'd gotten, but my buyer refused. The sentiment was "you are selling this as a finished, updated house and expecting top dollar for it—but if you didn't do the foundation work, what else didn't you do?" My contractor was even willing to complete the work during escrow at his own expense, but it was too late. My buyer walked. Now that I was fully aware of the problem, I was obligated to make the repairs before relisting the house. It ended up costing more than $10,000 and tacked an unwanted three weeks onto my time line. Worst of all, I had to pull it off the market, losing valuable exposure and shrouding the place with an air of mystery.

Once you have listed a property and gone into escrow and then fall out, it's almost impossible to get buyers and the agents representing them to notice you as an active, fresh listing again. There's confusion and gossip in the marketplace as to whether agents should show it because they heard it was in escrow, and then they heard it fell out because the *foundation crumbled*. When you have Realtor turmoil working against you, selling a flip can become an all-around nightmare.

The lesson: The minute you hire a contractor, go over all of the work that needs to be done and in what order. Jumping right into cosmetic repairs before the innards are upgraded is the flipping equivalent of rearranging the deck chairs on the RMS *Titanic*. When Santa Rosa's still-faulty foundation was discovered, I was furious. I felt that it was my contractor's job to take care of the mechanics while I focused on the aesthetics. After all, I had given him a copy of the physical inspection report I received when I purchased the property and highlighted the items I wanted him to repair. But the truth is, the buck always stops with the flipper. Even when you're paying someone else to be on top of things, the ultimate responsibility is yours.

Is it all worth while? Flipping is risky. It is all-consuming. It is fraught with disasters of every conceivable kind. When you hear about the buckets of money some people are making at it, don't be jealous. They're earning every penny, putting out one fire at a time.

As I write this book, I am helping my best friend Gina's dad renovate his house. Since I live 80 miles away from his property, Gina offered to help orchestrate some of the local activity. Because I am working with unknown vendors, I don't have those established, accountable relationships I continually highlight as being essential to a flip's success. An unavoidable instance in this case, but a detriment all the same.

Gina's first responsibility was to have a dumpster delivered so that work could begin promptly on Saturday morning. The dumpster arrived—but its 40-foot carcass was too big to fit in the driveway. A smaller dumpster was ordered, so you can imagine our surprise when a 60-foot replacement arrived on Monday. Three days later we had the right size receptacle. Just a week behind schedule.

Off to a great start, wouldn't you say? It happens. My best advice is to greet every day on every job with a cheerful "What else can go wrong?" A punch in the gut is always more bearable when you know it is coming. As my grandfather used to say, it's always best to prepare for the worst and be pleasantly surprised.

_____ Chapter Summary _____

1. **Don't unveil an experimental product.** Run every faucet, flush every toilet, test every fan before your first guest walks through the door. If something doesn't work perfectly, you want to find out before a potential buyer does.

2. **Know your breaking point.** Would you rather lose your life's savings or your sanity? Sometimes the best choice is merely the lesser of two evils. Flippers tread in risky waters and it is wise to know that before you dive in.

3. **Don't forget, you're the boss.** It is your job as the homeowner to manage your crew, and your right as the manager to cut loose anyone who doesn't meet your exacting standards. That's not cruel, it's smart business.

4. **Remain detached.** Getting emotionally tied to a house makes it hard to stick to the minimum in terms of improvements, and nearly impossible to attach a profitable price tag.

5. **Price your house right.** Your initial asking price should be just slightly lower than the amount comparable homes are selling for in your area. This will spark the greatest amount of interest and may generate multiple offers. If you're forced to lower your price, you're at a distinct disadvantage because you've lost the freshness that drives potential buyers through the front door.

10

ADJUSTING YOUR
MIND-SET

Flip·it·isms (flip-ə-´ti-zəms) *n.*   Soothing mantras
you will repeat to yourself over and over in an effort to
maintain your composure during the flipping process.

Mind-set. Attitude. Perspective. Besides being great
names for video games and racehorses, these three
elements are all critical components of your flip.
Being emotion-driven faculties, they'll fluctuate considerably
from day to day, even minute to minute over the course of the
project. But simply being aware of their role and importance
can boost your odds of success exponentially.

The cynics among you may be asking, "You're telling us that optimists will do better at this flipping business than pessimists?" Actually, yes. I'm not saying that picturing yourself rolling around on a mattress stuffed with cash will transform you into an instant millionaire or that on-the-job "smile therapy" will make you fall madly in love with construction if the reality is you'd rather bathe in molten lava than tighten a simple screw. What I am saying is that you will be faced with decisions, disappointments, and general disarray on a daily basis. Whether you realize it at the time, your reaction to each crisis is a conscious choice. When things go wrong, will you bark like a dog? Melt into a puddle? Kick, scream, and cry? Curse the unfairness of the universe? Or sigh and ask yourself, "What could I have done differently to avoid this situation?" and finally, "What did I learn from this experience and how can that knowledge benefit the rest of my life?"

It all begins with your attitude toward flipping in general. Is it a journey? An uncharted island you're excited to explore? A last resort? A get-rich-quick-and-easy scheme? Let me reiterate: Flipping houses is rarely quick and never easy. The folks who do it successfully earn every last penny they make. Recognizing that fact early on will save you resentment, disappointment, and ultimately, money. If you're not enamored with the flipping process, there are plenty of other ways to achieve financial success and personal satisfaction. You might start an eBay business, write a book, turn your home into a doggy day care, or join the Peace Corps.

What will your mind-set be when you buy the house, fix the house, and sell the house? Have you thought about what you will feel, think, and do?

Buying the House

For our purposes, let's suppose you understand all the risks and decide to make a commitment to see your flipping goals through. You painstakingly put your finances in order and, filled with excitement and eagerness, embark on the Great House Hunt. Days, weeks, maybe months go by until finally you find it: your underpriced, reeking-of-potential diamond in the rough. Giddy beyond belief, you pen the cleanest offer ever put down on paper, promising more than the asking price, agreeing to take the property as is, and volunteering to remove the dead animal carcasses in the backyard simply for the privilege of having your offer considered. You go home and celebrate your coup with a toast or two.

You're busy pouring another glass of bubbly when your real estate agent calls and informs you that you didn't get the house. Apparently there were 14 other offers, 10 of which were in some obscure way superior to yours.

Sure, you're disappointed. Losing a gem of a house feels like that moment when you're about to sneeze and then, for whatever reason, it simply vanishes. It's just like that—times a hundred zillion. It hurts. So now you have a choice: You can put all your energy into moping and whining and feeling sorry for yourself, or you can redirect it into something positive. You can have your agent request that your offer be put in a backup position. You can have a heart-to-heart with your agent to see if there is anything you could have done to make your offer stronger. Here's the part that stings: Honestly, sometimes there's nothing you could have done. The winning bidder may have been a friend of the seller, or she may have

177

written a gut-wrenching letter about how her grandfather built the house or how the property would be ideal for her handicapped daughter. The buyer might have just won the lottery and offered twice the asking price, or offered to let the seller stay in the master suite rent-free for the next 13 years. Some offers just cannot be beat.

When you lose out on a house, you can and must keep looking. You won't believe this at the time, but there will be another house. There always is. And ironically, the minute you find it, you'll probably get a call that the original property fell out of escrow and your backup offer has just been accepted.

I don't care what your religion is; you have to have faith to get into this game. When you get your heart set on a property that for whatever reason doesn't come through, 100 percent of the time a better one appears. If you take the "whatever is meant to be will be" approach, your heart and mind will be infinitely more open to the possibilities around you. If you lock yourself in your basement and stew over the "one that got away," it's not likely that a perfect replacement is going to come knocking at your door.

Because I have such extraordinary faith in you, I'm going to assume that when you miss an opportunity like this, you will have taken all my advice to heart and have continued the search. You lost out on Dump Number One, which was an agonizing blessing because you just landed Dump Number Two! It's bigger and better and it's all yours, and this time you actually wait until the closing day to over celebrate. You greet Day One raring to go. You may not realize it at the time, but your mind-set on this day will be critical to your success.

Fixing the House

Do you show up on time to meet your crew with a vat of fresh-brewed coffee, or do you blow in late and screech to a halt in the driveway, blocking the way and generally making life miserable for the dumpster-delivery guy? Are you empty-handed and confused, or do you arrive with a brand-new box of those nifty flat carpenters' pencils and several cans of marking paint so you can delineate precisely what is to be demolished? How prepared and professional you appear will have a direct impact on how fired up your crew will be. If you don't care, they certainly won't.

Once your dump has been demo'd, you begin orchestrating the overhaul. I can't overemphasize how easy it is to get swept up in a renovation frenzy. Remember, you chose this house for its inherent potential. It's vital to constantly ask yourself: "What were my impressions when I saw the house for the first time? What made me think I could fix it and re-sell it for a profit?" Trust the answers to those questions. Now that you've spent some time there, you may think that it needs more. You will start to scrutinize each room, and suddenly the charming wood floors will look scuffed and tired, and the perfectly paintable kitchen cabinets will be begging for early retirement. If you're not careful, the sledgehammer may start swinging itself all over the place without your conscious consent.

Put your personal preferences and your emotional attachment to the house aside and ask yourself: "How can I make the greatest return on this house?" If time and money grew on trees, just about any house could be breathtaking. But often, you'll realize the largest profit margin by simply cleaning up, repainting, and maybe throwing in some updated hardware and lighting. Most successful flippers can detach and put their egos aside.

Notice I said "most" and not "all." The truth is, I am not one of those flippers for whom less is more, and you might not be one either. For me, it's always been more important to see a property reach its full potential and gamble on getting rewarded for my hard work, sacrifice, and great taste than it is to make a quick buck. To offset this would-be weakness, I have put tremendous effort into finding and keeping an honest, reliable, conscientious crew and rewarding them handsomely. I've said it from the beginning: It is essential to know your strengths. If you're more interior decorator than business-minded tycoon, embrace that—but surround yourself with people who fill in your gaps.

My antiflipper mentality has paid off many times. I've had a lot of fun fueling a temporary spending habit and shopping to my heart's content for plasma TVs and elaborate sound systems my flip house did not need to sell, but I rationalized the spending by telling myself I could negotiate those extras separately when I sold the house. The right buyer even came along in those instances and rewarded me for my desire to overspend. My enthusiasm has also burned me. I overspent on outdoor fireplaces and imported stone that contributed to the final look of the house, but I probably would have made more money had I stuck with the necessary basics. Because it's my career and my passion and I always know there'll be another opportunity, I can afford to sacrifice the occasional windfall to preserve my pride or my reputation. That's a position I earned. If this is your first (or last) shot, if you're gambling with borrowed money you can't afford to lose, you need to stay the course.

Every day on every job, you must make conscious decisions. Before deciding whether something stays or goes (the
windows, the floors, the bathroom vanities, whatever), remind yourself that your goal is to turn a profit, and that if
you achieve that goal, there will be another flip. And possibly
another. If money is tight and you need to make a profit, do
what you can do this time and promise yourself that your
next flip—or the one after that—will be the one you submit to
Architectural Digest.

Here's a secret: Creating that to-die-for space is a bitter-
sweet victory. Unless you can afford to live in it (and budget-
busters rarely can), you're going to have to relinquish your
rights to it. Your buyer may very well come in and rip out the
beyond-perfect kitchen you lovingly designed because the
microscopic flecks in the granite give her a headache and she
finds stainless steel to be a tad cold. It is much easier to bid a
cheerful adieu to a nice-enough little home that's clean and
presentable and was conscientiously refurbished, especially
when the farewell is accompanied by a nice, fat check on closing day.

Once you are in possession of your property, you have as-
sumed the role of boss, even if you do not realize it. As such,
throughout the renovations, it is your responsibility to keep
the big picture in mind. I once worked with a flipper who
knew she wanted to create a space in her remodeled kitchen
for the refrigerator to appear built-in. I suggested she buy the
refrigerator first, and reminded her that the local appliance
store was having a huge sale that weekend. She ignored this
advice and gave her carpenter some rough measurements for
the opening. As you can probably predict, the refrigerator she
finally bought didn't fit into the opening. The poor contractor
had to frame it three times before he got it right. Had she

made the purchase immediately, she would have had a cut sheet delineating the exact measurements, saving time, money, and frustration. She also would have had one less item looming on her already too-long to-do list. Instead, she procrastinated, and it cost her. She couldn't have earned less respect from her contractor if she'd had "slacker" tattooed onto her forehead.

Proponents of the trickle-down theory in economics believe that when the government helps companies, they will produce more, thereby making more money and ultimately hiring more people and paying them better salaries. The employees, in turn, will have more money to spend, further stimulating the economy. I believe in a trickle-down theory of construction: Help your crew help you. Just because a meticulous job site is important to you, don't expect everyone who works for you to have the same priorities. Have a broom and some dustpans within arm's reach at all times and get in there yourself and do it. Hire a cleaning crew on heavy demo days so that the space stays organized. Far too often, untold hours are lost at job sites because the crews can't find their tools and materials in the disarray. Time literally is money on a flip and ultimately, the buck stops with you.

One of the best lessons I learned about this game came to me in the form of a completely undeserved gift from a client. Ethan had hired me to help him flip his house. Before work even commenced, he called me and began, "I know how hard you work and I'm grateful that you made time in your schedule for me. Is Thursday at 7:00 okay for a massage?" Do you think I charged him for every single hour I put in on the job? Do you think I didn't work harder and longer than I ever had in my life trying to live up to his expectations and earn his continued respect? The gesture he made was small, but incredibly impactful.

It is one thing to throw someone a bone for a job well done and quite another to pay it forward. I now begin every job by putting a hundred-dollar bill in my foreman's hand. I consider it a tip, as in *To Ensure Promptness.* A week later, I send out personal notes to everyone on my crew. "I wanted you to know that I noticed you picked up the trash that people were tripping over around the dumpster," I might write. "It's small contributions like that that will make this project a success for all of us. With gratitude, Kirsten." It feels great to acknowledge someone's efforts, and they're also much more likely to continue if they know that they are appreciated.

A note about notes: As with all communication, frequency begets brevity. In other words, the more often you articulate your desires and goals, disappointment, and approval, the less time you'll have to spend doing it. Make daily check-ins a habit, and be as receptive to criticism as you are to praise. If your crew members feel that they can't come to you with problems, they won't; and on a construction site, unspoken complaints and unsolved problems grow like cancers. Once you've made the decision to be a leader, lead you must.

PICTURE THIS

An effective way to communicate is with visual aids. Try using an enormous, easy-to-read, eye-catching chart. Seeing a running list of items that need to be completed encourages your crew by allowing them to see their progress on a daily basis. Seeing what has yet to be done also creates a sense of urgency that's essential to sticking to your time line.

Throughout your flip you will be challenged to keep a positive attitude. Your crew will discover that the rafters are covered with toxic mold. Or you will discover that a member of your crew is toxic, period. Although a neurotic freak-out is certainly apropos in either case, it's not going to do you any good. My advice: Don't be a victim, and don't give away your power. Your reaction is your choice, and your choices create your destiny. It is much more powerful to respond to a situation than to react to it. If you need to leave the heat of the moment, get a coffee, and reevaluate the problem, take the time to do so. A lot is at stake, and the way you handle that particular moment will set the tone for the duration of your flip.

When it comes to building snafus and their impact on your wallet, a contractor friend long ago convinced me to adopt a Zen approach: It's going to cost what it's going to cost, and it's going to take as long as it takes. That is a most frustrating reality, but once you accept it, you can move on. Discover your house has an asbestos issue? Instead of wasting your time being angry that your inspector didn't find it prior to closing escrow and being consumed by the escalation of your overhead, do your homework and stockpile competitive bids and choose the most qualified person offering the best deal to remove it. (Every nanosecond you're not doing this is costing you even *more* time and money.) All construction expenses boil down to labor and materials, so if you know what each is costing you and you are present on the job site to keep your crew gently but effectively motivated, you've done all that you can do. *It's going to cost what it's going to cost;* the implied but unspoken follow-up is, *and there's not a damned thing you can do about it.*

Except steadfastly plow on.

While toxic materials can be removed fairly easily, toxic people tend to pose a much greater challenge. Let's face it, we do this so we don't have to kiss up to a nasty boss, work in a hostile office, or perform an obligatory, unfulfilling task 40 or more hours a week. Whether it's TV, food, or relationships, if you put garbage in, you get garbage out. If you're surrounded by toxic people every day, you will eventually become toxic. There's just no way around it. Their negative energy will permeate every nonlead-based-paint-covered wall in your soul. If it's a toxic carpenter, fire him. A toxic partner, discuss buyout options. A toxic real estate agent, find another. A toxic spouse? Oh brother, get help quick. Poisonous people can make this journey, along with the rest of your life, utterly miserable.

The flip side, so to speak, is that this gig allows you to hand-select a group of people who share similar goals and interests. I urge you not to take this task lightly. Like attracts like, and the more scrupulous you are when assembling your team, the happier and more successful you will be during crunch time and beyond.

Throughout this book I've stressed the importance of finding and keeping a reliable crew. As much as that core group will be essential to your success, don't get complacent. Occasionally seek out a competitive bid, and be open to meeting new people who could add something to your team. When I first met my contractor Darrell, I had no way of knowing how long and fruitful our relationship would prove to be. Because of that experience, I look at every new person I meet as someone who might wind up having a huge impact on my life. Not every painter, plumber, or potential client I work with turns out to be a soul mate. But every once in a while, simply by being open to the possibility, I make a magical connection.

As the work begins to wind down, don't be surprised if patience is in short supply all around. The last days and weeks of a flip can be torturous. Everyone involved wants to see the finished result and is eager to complete the project. You may unintentionally become tyrannical toward your crew and begin insisting on all-nighters just to make your open house. Tolerance and wisdom may have all but vanished from your repertoire. I urge you to be patient. When you've come so far, resorting to mediocre work, or having an open house when the dumpster is still in the driveway or the place isn't staged just isn't worth it. I've greeted one too many open houses with raw hands from sanding and painting and moving for days straight, doing whatever it took to get the last of the finishing touches in place. During one particularly memorable open house, my custom sheers suddenly came crashing down because I made the quantum leap of faith it took to hang them with chewing gum, the only adhesive-like substance handy at 2:00 A.M. the night before. I share this humiliating anecdote because I hope it hammers home an important point: You only get one chance to make a splash. If the property isn't something you're proud to put your name on, postpone the sale. As painful as it sounds, you will be glad you did.

Selling the House

At no point in the game is your mind-set more important to the bottom line than that moment when all the work is complete and you're ready to sign the listing papers. In pricing your house, there's a fine line between motivation and greed. Yes, you worked hard; you took a huge risk, financially and emotionally; you managed unwieldy crews, wielded sophisticated tools, and learned more about faucets, fabrics, and finishes than you ever dreamed possible. You deserve to make money, just as your buyer deserves to purchase a lovingly renovated home at a reasonable price.

Here's the rub: The market will decide how much you take home, not you or your partner, or even your real estate agent. If you price your house too high, whether because you colossally overspent, listened to bad advice, became emotionally attached, or simply got greedy, your buyers will let you know *by not buying it.* What may sound like a sweeping generalization is a fact: Homes that are priced fairly always sell quickly; homes that are *not* priced fairly do not. When you overprice your house from the get-go, you cannot backpedal fast enough. That "price reduction!" banner on your ad doesn't scream "great deal"; it's code for "damaged goods." Buyers won't necessarily assume you asked too much for your property, but rather that there's something terminally wrong with it.

One leading online dictionary defines greed as "an excessive desire to acquire or possess more than what one needs or deserves." If you offer your home at a fair price you will get what you probably need and definitely deserve: A quick, successful close of escrow.

And what if that's not exactly how it goes down? How do you keep your chin up if despite your best efforts, your flipping experience was a complete and utter bust? Maybe you ran out of cash midflip and had to sell before you even got a chance to work your magic. Maybe you had all the time and the money in the world but it turned out the charming

Victorian you fell in love with couldn't be renovated after all because of special zoning requirements surrounding the sacred burial grounds it was built on, so you had to walk away. Or maybe your flip turned out perfectly, but the market happened to flop precisely 15 minutes before you hung your "For Sale" sign, and you wound up sitting on it for nine months before fire-selling it at a massive loss. Or your spouse got tired of being a construction-widow and jumped ship on the project and your marriage. I believe that even the darkest cloud has a silver lining. It might just take a while for the skies to clear before you can see it.

Everyone knows a person who, despite enduring difficult or even downright tragic circumstances, remains impossibly upbeat. The most magical of this breed seem to almost embrace their challenges. Shortly after the 1996 Olympics, America's number one and most beloved cyclist was diagnosed with testicular cancer so advanced that it had spread to his lungs and brain. Lance Armstrong later called his cancer "the best thing that ever happened to [him]." It wasn't the physical or emotional pain he treasured, or the devastation his body and his family suffered. It was what having a life-threatening illness taught him about the capacity of the human spirit that made him a better athlete and probably a better human being.

Be that guy (or gal). . . . Let every minute of every day of your flip and your life be a learning, growing experience. They say that what doesn't kill you makes you stronger. I've learned the hard way that this is true. Dig deep if you have to, but find that nugget of wisdom, that kernel of strength that didn't exist inside you before you embarked on this path. Hold onto it especially tightly if you're the type to bang your head on the wall to the tune of "What . . . was . . . I . . . *thinking?*" No one can predict whether you'll be richer or poorer at the end of a flip, but you will certainly be smarter. Some wild wacko with a knife can steal your car or your wallet, but your experiences and the wisdom they impart are yours to keep and no one can take them away.

CASE CLOSED

Win or lose, it's important to celebrate the closure or completion of a flip. I hope you'll be throwing a huge bash to thank all the amazing people who helped to make the project a shining success, but even if you're mourning a significant loss of money, time, or sanity, mark the occasion. Light a candle in a cupcake, schedule a massage, or simply raise a glass to your own chutzpah. Acknowledging yourself and that you took a huge, crazy risk might encourage you to bring what you learned on the journey into other areas of your life.

Chapter Summary

1. **Your attitude is a choice.** You have very little control over the inevitable mistakes, setbacks, and complications involved, but you have complete control over your reaction to them. Think of every job site as your

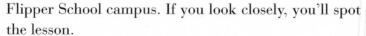

Flipper School campus. If you look closely, you'll spot the lesson.

2. **If you don't get the house, keep looking.** You will not always have enough money for the perfect property, and even if you can afford it and write a stellar offer, sometimes you will lose out to another buyer. Believe there's another gem around the next bend and it will appear.

3. **Your crew is a mirror of you.** Your behavior on and off the job site sends a powerful message to your team. If you expect punctuality, professionalism, and respect, lead by example.

4. **Remember your first impression.** What positive impression did you see when you first walked through the front door? In most cases, you'll realize the biggest profit by doing simple fixes. Repairing almost always costs less than replacing.

5. **Pay it forward.** Don't always wait for your crew to do something spectacular before rewarding them. Few things are more motivating than a bonus doled out up front.

6. **Don't rush to the finish.** As your project winds down, don't sacrifice quality just to meet an arbitrary deadline. Make sure to leave enough time for an inspection. You don't want to overlook something your new buyers might discover during *their* inspection that could blow your deal.

7. **Put the kibosh on greed.** You deserve to make a profit. Your buyer deserves a nice home at a reasonable price. Strike that balance when you price your home and everyone wins.

11

FREQUENTLY ASKED QUESTIONS

Flip·a·the·tic (flip-ə-´the-tik) *adj.*   At a loss for the answers when it comes to flipping efficiently.

My primary reason for writing this book is that every day I receive letters and e-mails asking for my advice on flipping. This chapter is a compilation of FAQs—quick, straightforward answers to the questions people ask with the greatest frequency. I have covered many of the following questions elsewhere in this book, often in greater detail. Nevertheless, this chapter is a handy refresher even if you have read and digested every word I've written up until now. If you're one of those "gimme the bottom line" folks who skipped straight to this chapter, consider it an appetizer. If you're hungry for more, you'll find plenty of meat in the main course that is the rest of this book. Bon appétit!

How Do I Get Started?

You're already on your way, just by picking up this book. The first steps are to get your finances in order, clean up your credit if necessary, get to know your local real estate market intimately, and start meeting with lenders. If you begin house-hunting without really knowing what you can buy or how much you can afford, or if you're up to your eyeballs in debt and can no longer answer your phone for fear it may be a creditor trying to hunt you down, you're wasting time. As eager as you are to jump right in, you have to do your home-work. If you skipped straight to this section and are serious about flipping, I encourage you to go back and read Chapter 3 for step-by-step instructions.

Do I Need Any Special License or Skills to Flip Houses?

The short answer is No. A real estate license may save you money if you know the market, can remain detached enough to price your house for a quick yet profitable sale, and under-stand how to get your flip the maximum amount of exposure and traffic. You don't have to be a contractor or a plumber, although any related ability that you possess and can con-tribute, from paint prep to tile setting, will directly affect your bottom line. The most important skill in this game, and one that everyone has, is the ability to question. Research, research, and then research some more. Talk to financial professionals, set up informational interviews, become an expert on your state and local real estate laws and regulations. Talk to people who have done it successfully as well as those who have flopped. In this business, ignorance is the polar opposite of bliss.

How Will I Know How Much Money I Can Make on a Flip?

Consult your trusty Magic 8 Ball like I do? Okay, you can't. But you can—and must—make an educated guess by using historical comparisons, facts, and figures to predict a reasonable sales price. From that point, you can work backward to create a detailed budget; the remainder is your alleged profit before fees (see Chapter 5 for all of the nitty gritty details on determining your profit margin).

If The Market Seems to Be Changing, Is Now Still a Good Time to Flip Houses?

Flipping is passé! Real estate is yesterday's investment! (But I've got a nice hunk of gold bullion for sale. . . .) Everyone has an opinion, and mine is that anti-real estate negativity is unfounded, uneducated fear. If you buy the right house at the right price, it's always a good time to flip—and I'd love to see a shred of proof to the contrary. Remember my restaurant analogy (see Chapter 1). Just as there will invariably be folks who would rather have their food prepared for them than do it themselves, there will always be buyers looking for a home in move-in condition. In an unrealistically robust market, as we saw in the recent past, flippers could make a healthy profit by sheer appreciation. In a more normal market, as we're seeing today, you must increase your home's value to see a return on your investment. Today more than ever, you make money on the buy, and you find the right house by staying on top of your local market conditions and knowing what is out there at all times. When you've been to 200 open houses in 20 weeks, you'll learn how to spot a steal and jump on it. Pick up that diamond in the rough for a song and you'll be singing all the way to the bank!

How Can I Avoid a Multiple-Offer Situation When I Go to Purchase My Flip?

Multiple-offer situations aren't a bygone product of the real estate boom of the recent past; if the house is a great deal, there should and will be multiple offers. This is where it is critical to work with an experienced, knowledgeable agent. Once you determine the maximum amount you are willing to pay, she can help you write the strongest possible offer. With a little finesse and a lot of luck, you may just get the property. And if you don't, there's another house out there with your name on it—you just have to go out and find it.

What Does "Creative Financing" Mean?

Creative financing can mean just about anything from using borrowed or stolen money, securing multiple loans, or applying for multiple credit cards and then maxing them out. Lenders are in on the game, offering negative amortization loans (where you pay only a portion of the interest and the rest gets tacked onto the principal) and longer (40-year) loans that make monthly payments lower and therefore more affordable in the short term. In the best sense, creative financing means doing whatever you need to do within sensible and legal limits to get into the game. If you're paying 20 percent interest to borrow $100,000 from a loan shark, you're paying $1,666 a month in interest alone that has to be factored into your carrying costs. In that case, you need to make absolutely sure that you bought that house enough under market value to absorb your costs. Borrowed money is expensive, but it's a risk most flippers must be willing to take.

What Are My Options If I Run Out of Money?

You have several options although few of them are particularly attractive. You can abandon ship and sell the property as is. You can find a partner who can invest time and/or money to help you finish the improvements. Is moving in a possibility? It might be if you're paying rent elsewhere, or your own house is more marketable. Whatever the case, if you find yourself in this situation, you can bet you're going to have to make some sacrifices. A brilliant man I know says the problem in this country (he's from Ireland) is that Americans spend money we don't have on things we don't need to impress people we don't know. Part of the issue is that many of us can no longer distinguish our needs from our wants. We're spoiled. She "needs" a manicure every week. He "needs" a $4 coffee every morning. Serve yourself a healthy dose of tough love instead. It seems impossible, but many of us could learn to live without gym memberships, designer clothes, fancy foreign cars, milkshakes disguised as coffee drinks, cable TV, semiweekly tee times, video rentals, and the latest digital wireless phone/camera/forklift combo. If you tallied up your frivolous expenses each week, you'd probably be floored by the total. Determine where you can cut back, and then do it dramatically. Consider it a short-term investment in your long-term happiness and financial stability.

What Are My Options If My Flip Doesn't Sell Immediately?

If you weren't wise or brave enough to underprice it from the beginning—a strategy employed to generate interest and often, multiple offers—you have two options: Wait it out or lower your price. This is where your math skills, once again, will be called on. If your carrying costs are $5,000 a month and it takes six months to get your current asking price, that's $30,000 from your bottom line. If it sits empty for a year, that's $60,000. Could you lower it by $10,000 and sell it today? I worked with one flipper on the show who actually listed his house for considerably less than he had into it, and well below market value. He received 17 offers, a bidding war ensued, and in the end he wound up getting $50,000 over his asking price. It's a risky tactic but one worth considering, especially if a quick sale is more important to you than holding out for a lofty sticker price. In Santa Barbara, where I live, if I haven't received a single offer within three weeks, I know it's time to reexamine my price. Rather than dropping my price a nickel this week and a dime the next, if I'm sitting on a stagnant property, I usually go straight to my breakeven point. Sometimes it's best to dump it and move on.

I Don't Have a Lot of Money. Should I Flip a House with a Partner?

Of all the questions I'm asked, none terrifies me as much as this one. I liken flipping partnerships to marriage: They're not to be entered into lightly. Some work out swimmingly and the parties become closer and stronger for the experience; some end in a courtroom with nasty looks and the smack of a gavel. Yes, having a partner or partners minimizes your financial risk. Ostensibly, each partner also brings some unique skill or talent into the fold that lowers your bottom line, but the saying, "Too many cooks spoil the broth" is also appropriate here. If you have four partners, four distinct personalities may be weighing in on each and every decision. How will you decide who wins? How will you handle the hurt or angry feelings of the partner or partners whose suggestions are rejected? How will you divide the work? The profits or losses? Who is the chief and who are the Indians? Is everyone okay with the arrangement? Do you have a plan in place for unexpected events, such as one partner wanting out or another wanting to move in? If you enter into a partnership, treat it as a business and proceed accordingly. And get everything in writing, even if your partner is a family member. Especially if your partner is a family member.

Is There Any Way to Avoid the Tax Ramifications of Making Money on a Flip?

If you make a profit, it's considered income, a portion of which you are required by law to pay in the form of income tax. Because you can deduct every last penny of your related expenses from your taxable profits, it may be worth your time and money to sit down with a real estate attorney. If you contributed to the labor, you may be able to pay yourself a salary. That sum would be added to your cost basis and therefore decrease your taxable total. This is another reason that it is crucial to keep track of your expenses and your receipts. If you're into this for the long haul, you can roll your profits into another house and avoid paying capital gains tax with a nifty little tool called a 1031 Exchange. Look for a firm that specializes in this type of transaction if you plan to flip again soon. You might also consider embarking on a pattern of buying and selling every two years. In this scenario, you move into your flip—maybe even doing the renovations while you're living there to avoid shelling out a rent or a mortgage payment elsewhere—and then sell once the capital gains tax period has expired.

Do You Have Any Tips for Staying Organized?

A CPA I am not, but I do know that how well you manage your finances during a flip will directly contribute to your success or failure. Whether you use a shoebox or sophisticated software, you must keep track of every expense. Each time you purchase even a simple roll of adhesive tape, write on the back of the receipt what it was for. As soon as possible, enter the item and amount into whatever system you have established. Create a way to distinguish bills that have been reconciled with bills that have not. Make posting, tracking, and reviewing your expenses a daily activity; there's no better way to keep things from falling through the cracks. Plus with daily check-ins, there's little chance that you will let your whole budget get out of hand without realizing it. I have fooled myself into thinking I'm spending considerably less than I actually am just by doing rough addition in my head for the big-ticket items. Likewise, the accumulation of a thousand tiny expenses can blow a budget in the blink of an eye. So many flippers take the "out of sight, out of mind" approach. They lose receipts, keep track of nothing and just sort of cross their fingers that everything will work out in the end. These are typically the folks that dramatically overspend and then dramatically overprice. They're also rarely the runaway success stories. If you're on top of your project financially, you can put on the brakes as necessary.

How Can I Keep My Team on Their Toes?

Other than being present physically, your next best tool is to hold weekly meetings. Not only does this keep tasks prioritized and people organized, but it adds an essential element of accountability. Discuss the week's agenda and tell your crew what you expect to be completed each day. I like to offer incentives such as an extra $20 or $50 or an afternoon off (with or without pay) for a task done quickly *and* well. That last bit is key; it's never worth it to sacrifice quality for a quick turnaround.

Are There Any Concerns That Apply Specifically to Condos?

In expensive or inflated areas, condos can be a great point of entry into the real estate market. Because they're governed by a group of homeowners, they also come with their own set of rules and regulations. The *covenants, conditions, and restrictions* (CC&Rs) may also be known by another name, such as the *bylaws* or *master deed.* These documents spell out the rules that each of the condo owners—as well as their tenants and guests—must obey. The condo association rules may dictate whether you can add a deck, install a skylight, put up a fence, or change the front door. You might have to seek the approval of 27 neighbors before you switch your trim paint from white to ivory. You may need to factor additional fees and dues into your carrying costs, as well as annoyances like parking and trash restrictions. Because of their relative affordability, condos can be a great place to start—as long as you know exactly what you're getting into and plan accordingly.

I'm Running out of Time and Money. Can I Schedule an Open House Even Though Everything Isn't Finished?

Can you take a nap on the local train tracks wearing earplugs or look down the barrel of a loaded gun? Absolutely—but I beg, plead, and implore you not to do that. You have one chance to make a first impression. The whole point of flipping is to get paid a premium for a finished product. If you list your house in a state of semireadiness, you're throwing away money. You cannot put a price on the emotional pull of offering a house that contains everything but the buyer's toothbrush. Please, finish the job you started (see the earlier question about options when you're maxed out). Your pride and your wallet will thank you.

How Do You Know When to Splurge and When to Do the Minimum?

Nine times out of ten, you can save yourself boatloads of time and effort by just doing basic cosmetic repairs. Additions, major renovations, and complete overhauls are extremely expensive and time consuming. Even though you can ask considerably more for your finished product, the added expense of the materials and your carrying costs might negate any profit. Remember, time equals money. If you can get a product or service cheaply—your brother makes custom cabinets, your best friend is an appliance wholesaler and gets everything at cost—by all means include it. When you save money, you make money. Otherwise, you'll probably be better off in the end if you stick to the basics.

I Went Hog Wild with My Renovations and Plan to Price My House Accordingly. I Deserve It, Right?

While you can decide how much you're going to ask for your house, the market will tell you in no uncertain terms how much it will pay. The best thing that can happen to you is that you get two or more buyers to bid against each other, and the most effective way to do that is to price your house fairly for your neighborhood. "Buy the worst house on the best block," isn't just advice for flippers; no one wants to buy a mansion in the slums. Keep that in mind when plowing ahead with your renovations.

Do I Need to Get Permits for All the Work I'm Going to Do?

In some areas, technically, you need a permit for anything that costs over $500. Yes, work can be done without permits—but if you're caught doing it, you'll wind up paying more in the form of penalties and fees. Don't be intimidated by the permitting process; although occasionally it can be complicated, costly, and time-consuming, sometimes it's a matter of filling out a quick form and going about your business. Do I like the process and enjoy dishing out that money personally? Of course not. But your potential buyer might be a rule-freak who walks away because you didn't do it the right way. Think of getting your necessary permits as one less thing to keep you up at night.

What Are the Critical Elements in a Finished Flip?

That depends on the area or neighborhood you live/ flip in. If all your neighbors have high-end stainless steel appliances, dual showerheads in the master bath and front- and rear-yard sprinkler systems, you need to have them, too. In fact, ideally your finished flip should be one step ahead of what people are already doing or buying in the area. Think of features and amenities you can easily and inexpensively incorporate into your house while the renovations are underway. Adding automatic closet lights, prewiring your walls for Internet/plasma connections or putting rope lighting around your floorboards or underneath your countertops might be the touch that nudges you ahead of your competition.

What Is the Key to Creating a Realistic Time Line?

The more extensive your renovations, the harder it is to estimate how long each element and project will take. Conversely, the longer you do it and the more experienced you become, the better you will get at allocating your time. Construction is a complicated business and mistakes happen constantly. Materials get lost, broken, and misdelivered. Pipes break, windows crack, cabinets get hung upside down. (No lie. This recently happened to some friends who were flipping their first house.) People don't show up when they're supposed to. My best advice is to plot your course carefully, then expect the worst, hope for the best and be pleasantly surprised when things actually go as planned!

Do I Really Need to Stage My Flip?

Houses are like bodies: They tend to look better dressed. Without furnishings and decor, even the loveliest home is nothing but some walls flanked by a floor and a ceiling. Let your potential buyers see how the space is best utilized, and help them imagine what it would feel like to come home there at the end of the day. Home-buying is emotional stuff, and staging is one of the best ways to draw your buyers in.

Real Estate Commissions Are So High—Can I Just Do It Myself and Save the Money?

You would think so, wouldn't you? In most cases, you would be wrong. According to a recent article in the *Los Angeles Times* (April 23, 2006), FSBOs (For Sale by Owners) earn 16 percent less than owners of comparable homes who put the sale in the hands of an experienced real estate agent. (The study cited was conducted by the National Association of Realtors, which surveyed 7,813 buyers and sellers to arrive at that figure.) Your agent will do a lot more than fill out some complex paperwork on your behalf. She will do all the marketing for your home, help you price your house effectively, weigh in on staging decisions and hold open houses. She also has access to her entire group of peers, many of whom already have buyers on the hook waiting to jump on that perfect property. Just as you certainly wouldn't perform open-heart surgery on yourself or try to fix your broken-down car if you didn't know an alternator from an ashtray, some endeavors are simply better left to the pros.

So... Should I Do This or Not?

If you're ready for adventure, aren't afraid of a little risk, and wouldn't be devastated if you didn't make enough money to fund your immediate retirement, come on in—the water's great!

Why Would You Write a Book on Flipping If You're a Flipper? Aren't You Afraid of the Competition?

If you are bold enough to embark on this journey, you're not my competition, you're my inspiration. You may have realized by now that I don't do this for the money, although that is certainly a nice perk. I do it for the personal satisfaction and for the way it enriches every area of my life. When people set out to succeed, they are often in search of fame and fortune. Those are noble enough endeavors, but not nearly as important as the next and, to me, most important step: philanthropy. When you reach a place where giving feels better than getting, in my opinion you have it all. Giving actually ends up being pretty selfish—because it makes you feel so good.

Flipbonics

Back·flip (ˈbak-flip) *n.*   The move you'll perform the day you get your first full-price offer.

Flip·aer·o·bics (flip-er-ˈō-biks) *n.*   The grueling workout you get during a flip.

Flip·a·li·cious (flip-ə-ˈli-shəs) *adj.*   A tastefully completed flip.

Flip·a·the·tic (flip-ə-ˈthe-tik) *adj.*   At a loss for answers when it comes to making the most out of a flip.

Flip·hap·py (ˈflip-ha-pē) *adj.*   Refers to the euphoric feeling generated by a successful flip that leads you to purchase another fixer-upper.

Flip·ol·o·gy (flip-ˈäl-ə-jē) *n.*   The study of flipping property.

Flip·o·mat·ic (flip-ə-ˈma-tik) *adj.*   Descriptive of a quick and easy flip.

Flip·o·me·ter (flip-ˈä-mə-tər) *n.*   A handy tool used by flippers for daily mental check-ins.

Flip·o·suc·tion (ˈflip-ə-sək-shən) *n.*   The paring of a house down to its bare bones.

Flip·per·op·ol·is (flip-ər-ˈäp-ə-lis) *n.*   A city or area with a heavy concentration of flippers.

Flip·per·os·i·ty (flip-ər-ˈäs-ɪ-tē) *n.*   The sharing of flipping tips with others.

Flip·shape (ˈflip-shāp) *adj.*   Used to describe the near-perfect homes that conscientious flippers attempt to create.

Freu·di·an flip (ˈfröi-dē-ən flip) *n.*   The mistake of renovating a property so that it closely resembles the home of your ex or your mother.

Photos of Flips

(Before)

An undefined space in the corner of the master bedroom.

(After)

Exterior windows remain in place as this office is transformed into a master bathroom.

(Before)

This empty living room lacks emotional pull and a feeling of "home."

(After)

The room is updated with new paint, window treatments and furnishings, enabling potential buyers to picture themselves in this staged home.

(Before)

A master bedroom in need of a closet and cohesive design.

(After)

The space is greatly improved with the addition of a walk-in closet (behind the bed wall) and upholstered headboard.

(Before)

A dated bathroom with poor use of space.

(After)

The new layout and updated finishes in this luxurious master bath make the difference between getting top dollar and no sale at all!

(Before)

A blank and boring bedroom.

(After)

The room has been transformed into an elegant master suite with the addition of crown molding, window coverings, hardwood floors, and luxurious furnishings.

(Before)

A useless wall cuts off the kitchen from the living room.

(After)

Structurally the same, but a pop out, new counter top, paint, and window coverings create the feeling of an expansive space.

Index

217

Interviews, for contractors,
66–67

Junk fees, waiving, 60

Kemp, Kirsten, 9–20, 206
as actress, 12–13
death of father, 15–16
as flipper, 16–20
as interior designer, 13–14,
15–16, 18–19, 50
marriage of, 17
qualifications of, 9–10
as student, 13–16
this book and, 20, 206
Kitchen, renovation of, 110,
111, 123, 124, 129
Kitchen appliances, staging
with, 154–155
Knowing oneself, house flipping
and, 49–52

Laguna Street fixer-upper, 165
Landscaping, 136–137
Lawns, 136–137
Lawn sprinkler systems,
136–137
Lawyers. *See* Attorneys
Learning experience:
house flipping as, 4–6,
161–163, 188–189
of Kirsten Kemp, 13–20,
49–52

Lenders:
appraisals and inspections
and, 82–84
creative financing and, 195
finding good, 58–65, 74
usefulness of, 28–29
License:
for contractor, 70, 192
for realtor, 53, 192–193
"Lick and stick" experts, 7
Liens, by contractors, 70
Lifestyle accents, accessories as,
154
Limited liability companies
(LLCs), 64
Living room, renovation of,
114, 116, 128, 211
Loans, 23–25. *See also*
Financing
interest-free, 62
negative amortization, 62
prepayment penalties for, 63
promotional programs for,
62
stated asset stated income,
64
30-year fixed, 62
Location, in house flipping,
32–34
Lockbox, 56–57
London Interbank Offered Rate
(LIBOR), 64
Lowballing, 36, 40–43